Creatively CHRISTMAS

Inspired Yuletide Decor

Jennifer RIZZO

Creatively CHRISTMAS

Inspired Yuletide Decor

Jennifer RIZZO

PLAIN SIGHT PUBLISHING
AN IMPRINT OF CEDAR FORT, INC.
SPRINGVILLE, UTAH

The author of this book strives to be as original as possible and provide content as original as possible. Any project resemblance to any project previously published is purely coincidental.

The projects featured in this book are not intended for children. Some projects and supplies may be a choking or strangulation hazard. All mantel projects are intended for a nonworking fireplace and may be flammable. Please use proper safety precautions when attempting projects, and all book projects are at reader's own risk.

ISBN 13: 978-1-4621-1424-5

Published by Plain Sight Publishing, an imprint of Cedar Fort, Inc.
2373 W. 700 S., Springville, UT 84663
Distributed by Cedar Fort, Inc., www.cedarfort.com

LIBRARY OF CONGRESS CATALOGING-IN-PUBLICATION DATA

Rizzo, Jennifer, 1982-, author.
Creatively Christmas / Jennifer Rizzo.
     pages cm
Includes index.
Summary: A Christmas craft tutorial with each chapter focusing on a different area of the home. Includes homemade decorative gift-wrap tape and handmade gifts.
ISBN 978-1-4621-1424-5
1. Christmas decorations. 2. Handicraft. I. Title.

TT900.C4R538 2014
745.594'12--dc23

                    2014023815

Cover and page design by Angela D. Baxter
Cover design © 2014 by Lyle Mortimer.
Edited by Deborah Spencer

Printed in the United States of America

10 9 8 7 6 5 4 3 2 1

Printed on acid-free paper

DEDICATION

This book is dedicated to my amazing husband and children. Thank you so much for loving me and supporting me and being the most beautiful gift I've ever received.

"**JENNIFER RIZZO** has contributed creative projects to *Romantic Homes* and her home has been featured in one of our holiday issues. Her book, *Creatively Christmas*, has much of the same vintage-inspired and creative ideas used in new and modern ways. It's holiday inspiration from cover to cover."

Jacqueline deMontravel, editor, *Romantic Homes* magazine

"**THE CLASSIC, APPROACHABLE** style that Jennifer Rizzo is known for in the blog world comes alive on the pages of this beautiful book. The projects will awaken your creativity and inspire you to DIY your way to a stunning holiday home."

Marian Parsons, blogger Miss Mustard Seed and author of *Inspired You: Breathing New Life into Your Heart and Home*

"**DURING MY TIME** as an editor at *Country Living*, Jen and I collaborated on craft projects as well as a feature on her amazing kitchen renovation. Not only does she have a great eye for DIY and design, but Jen's ideas are also approachable and inspiring to people with all types of DIY experience. Plus, everything she creates is majorly budget-friendly. Score!"

Jourdan Fairchild, former crafts editor of *Country Living* magazine, freelance writer/editor, author of *Fly DIY*

"**CREATIVELY CHRISTMAS** is what the holidays are all about for us! As the children have gotten older, we have learned that a slower, simpler, and more handmade Christmas fits the heart of our home. Jennifer Rizzo has created a gorgeous book that brings the holidays back to the simple and beautiful details that we all want the holidays to be about."

Jeanne Oliver, artist and owner of the Jeanne Oliver Creative Network and blogger

"**I'VE KNOWN JEN** for over six years. She has never failed to inspire and this book is no exception. A visual delight for the senses from cover to cover, *Creatively Christmas* will make you want to celebrate Christmas year round. From her exquisite photography to her innovative projects, Jennifer Rizzo proves once again she is a designer who is here to stay."

KariAnne Wood, blogger at *Thistlewood Farm*

"**JENNIFER RIZZO'S** creativity knows no bounds, which shines through in her book, *Creatively Christmas*. From gifts to decorating, every page is full of inspiration to get you in the holiday spirit and embrace the holiday the handmade way."

Gina Luker, blogger at *The Shabby Creek Cottage* and author of *How to Start a Home-based Etsy Business*

"**JEN HAS** amazed us for years with her one-of-a-kind style, thoughtful attention to detail, and beautiful creations. Be prepared to be wowed by this collection of inspiring projects by a true artist at the core."

Jamin and Ashley Mills, Bloggers at the *Handmade Home* and authors of *Handmade Walls: 22 Inspiring Ideas to Bring Your Walls to Life*

CONTENTS

A VERY VINTAGE
CHICAGO CHRISTMAS

XI

A VERY VINTAGE CHICAGO CHRISTMAS

MY EARLIEST HOLIDAY memories revolve around our huge, extended, Polish family getting together in my great-aunt's basement. She lived with her sister in a one-hundred-year-old two-flat: she and her husband on the top floor, her sister and her sister's husband on the bottom. My grandmother lived across the street and a few other relatives were scattered down the lane as well. It was the kind of Chicago city street with old brick and clapboard houses, with parking so scarce you used old chairs to save your parking space, and it was an unwritten rule that you never moved someone's chair and just parked in that spot.

On Christmas Eve, around 4 p.m., my parents, my brothers, and I would head out to the "city" from our little house in the 'burbs. The older relatives considered it "the country" back then. We would all get together, the cousins, the aunts, and the uncles smooshed together in the wood-raftered brick basement. After climbing down some treacherously steep stairs, we would sit at long wooden bingo tables on hard metal folding chairs borrowed from the church and eat and talk, all while basking in the light of the white metal Christmas tree adorned with plastic fruit. The tree had a color wheel that would spin around and around and change the tree from red to blue and green.

Before we would eat, we followed an old Polish tradition called Opłatki. It's a thin, airy unleavened wafer that we would get about a cracker-size piece of. We would go around the room greeting each other. We would break off a piece of the other person's cracker, they would break off a piece of ours, and then we would eat the pieces and wish each other a blessed new year with a hug and a kiss.

PHOTO BY JIM BONK

Once the holiday blessings were done, we would eat some great Polish staples, or what we like to refer to jokingly as "gray and brown food": pierogi, mushroom soup, sausage, rye bread, sauerkraut, and potatoes. We would stuff ourselves until we were full, knowing that dessert was going to be served as soon as the plates were washed in the two huge concrete sinks in the corner and the tables were cleared. We would sneak up to the tree, try to see if a present had our name on it, and then dash away when one of the adults caught us peeking.

After dessert and coffee, we put our pajamas on and played while we were waiting for Santa. When Santa came, we would each get one gift to open and then try to figure out who he was this year. One year I was positive it was my Uncle Sandy, only to find him standing next to me, and me a little freaked out that maybe it was the real Santa.

After Santa, the adults would drink their coffee, have more dessert, and play a card game called Pinochle. (They sounded like they were having so much fun eating cookies, laughing, and playing, with the occasional knock and crowd roar.)

Then, at some point, all of the food would come back out again and we'd have a second dinner, the kids would wind down, and everyone would start to say their good-byes. In the cold, we'd pile into our station wagon and head back out to the suburbs. It was the 1970s and my brothers and I would lie in the back under blankets and count the streetlights as they passed overhead. At that time on Interstate 55 there were these really cool blue streetlights and we were enthralled by them. I'd watch them zip by one by one, and suddenly, our car would be stopped, I would be opening my eyes, and I would be home.

Sometime in my teen years, the family became just too big and the aunties too old and we broke off into smaller family groups. As I grew older, I missed those big, crazy parties, but I realized as family changes, Christmas changes. Life changes.

As everyone grew older, as it happens in a big family, every few years or so someone would pass away and the space they left would be a gaping realization that they wouldn't be here forever.

For me, as I grow older and have a family of my own, it becomes less about "the stuff" and more about the family and my faith.

The season for me becomes so much more about memories I have and making new ones that my children will remember, because I know that that is what they will have to hold onto when they are my age. They will look back and remember how we spent the most important holiday of all, and they will hopefully be making new traditions for themselves and their families.

In all those years, I don't remember many of the presents I received. But what I do remember are the feelings, and the people, and all of the things that didn't seem important at the time, but are so important now.

I love decorating and fussing for the holidays. I love the singing and the music, the snow and holiday movies, baking cookies, the greenery and lights. I adore the excitement that I know my children are going to have on Christmas morning, but even more than these, I love that we are making new memories and traditions for them. As a family, we attend Christmas Eve Service. It's my favorite of all. It's a beautiful service celebrating the birth of our Savior, Jesus Christ. At the end of the service the entire congregation stands around the manger and sings Silent Night together as one church family. Afterward, we head home, where I cook a "gray and brown" feast just for us and the kids get to open one gift each. The next day is spent bopping between family and getting ready for the 26th. That is the new tradition for us. Since Christmas Eve has been parceled off to different family groups, we make an effort to have all of the cousins over for pizza and just get together, enjoying each other's company and making a memory that I hope my own children will be able to store up for themselves.

CHAPTER 1

WINTER WONDERLAND

WEATHERPROOF PRESENTS

BY WRAPPING shipping boxes in plastic sheeting, found at the fabric store for a few dollars a yard and secured with heavy-duty tape, you can make a merry display.

Where tree tops glisten

IF WIND is an issue, a plastic bag with sand in the bottom box can help keep the gifts weighted against winter weather.

AFTER WRAPPING tightly in plastic and tape, use lightweight quilting fabric and heavy-duty clear tape along with plastic ornaments to decorate the boxes.

REPURPOSED ICE SKATES

FOUND IN thrift stores and at garage sales for a few dollars a pair, they can dress up a fence when paired with a simple pine garland or a vintage sled.

ICE SKATES too worn to wear can still have a second life as holiday decor.

WINTER WONDERLAND

5

SNOWBALL TOPIARIES

I THOUGHT IT WOULD BE FUN to have planters full of snowballs all winter long no matter how hot the sun was. The secrets to the sparkly "snowballs" are shatterproof ornaments that have foam instead of plastic as a base. Just use caution when pushing the skewers into the foam so you make a hole in the foam and not yourself.

Gather

Garden planters

Approx. 2 yards burlap

10-inch white craft foam cones

Craft foam balls (white), 6 inches, 4 inches, and 2 inches

Bamboo skewers

Small-diameter knitting needle

Hard foam-based shatterproof glitter ornaments

1. **PLACE THE WHITE** craft foam cone in the planter, padding the inside with burlap to help hold it in place. Depending on the size of your urn v. foam you may need to use more foam.

2. **CUT THE FOAM** off about 3 inches from the top so there is a wider top.

3. **PREPOKE A HOLE** in the 6-inch foam balls and glitter ornaments with a small diameter knitting needle and add some all-purpose glue into the hole. Carefully insert the bamboo skewers into the foam balls; one end will be sharp. They may also need to be trimmed to shorter lengths depending on how far up the foam base you are going.

4. **ADD GLUE TO** the skewer end and, starting at the base of the cone nearest the planter opening, insert it into the cone. Build your snowballs from the bottom up, ending up with a glitter ball at the top. Use smaller foam balls to fill in any gaps or open spots.

DON'T FORCE the skewers in—that could mean a greater chance at slipping and poking yourself.

Tip

Buy your foam balls
in bulk. They can be
pricey buying them
one at a time.

IF YOU CAN'T find glitter
ornaments, glitter your own with a
weatherproof glue.

WINTER WONDERLAND

9

CHAPTER 2

A MERRY HELLO

FRONT DOOR AND PORCH DECORATING IDEAS

A FARMHOUSE porch gets an unconventional eye-catching display of red and green with pine boughs and a vintage book.

THIS PORCH gets touches of color with symmetrical wreaths and planters that give a festive welcome from the street.

THE WREATH on the front door is a nice repeat to tie the porch and entry together.

A VINTAGE pink trunk adds a nice touch of unexpected color.

A MERRY HELLO

13

A VINTAGE chicken nesting box holds birch logs and vintage lunch boxes.

WITH GREENERY and lights following the original window above the door, it makes a welcoming entry accented with berries.

AN ANTIQUE ice bucket is the perfect place for a woodsy display.

A GALVANIZED bucket stenciled with "etc." holds extra greenery.

A LIVING TREE in an urn can be used year-round and planted later when it outgrows the planter.

A DISPLAY of pinecones and concrete ornaments can stay out long past Christmas.

A PORCH dressed to the nines makes a welcoming entry for holiday guests with a place to enjoy the snowy view.

15

SANTA'S MAIL BAG

I STARTED MAKING THESE BAGS a few years ago when I started wholesaling my home decor to retail shops. People loved them so much, I couldn't keep up with them. I had to share because I think that this has so many uses and is so cute!

This project involves using solvent image transfer, which sounds scary but is easy. I use a product called Citrasolv. It's a natural, environmentally friendly cleaner/degreaser made from oranges and has a ton of other uses. When you're done with your artwork, you can clean the bathtub! If you visit their website you can see many of the art projects people use it for. Even though it's a natural cleaner, I still recommend using it in a well-ventilated room and using proper safety precautions (I also generally wear gloves and eye protection). Please visit their website, listed at the back of this book, if you have any questions about the product or any other questions on how to use it for art projects.

Gather

Canvas gear bag

Citrasolv all-purpose cleaner/degreaser

Cotton balls

Latex gloves

Painter's tape

Wood craft stick

Brown ink pad

Black-and-white images or printables provided

1. **GET YOUR BLACK-AND-WHITE** images ready. They need to be reversed from how you want them to appear. They also need to be printed on a printer with toner, like a copy machine. Ink jet prints will not work.

2. **LAY YOUR BAG** flat and tape prints to where you want them to be transferred. Lightly saturate a cotton ball with Citrasolv and lightly wipe it over the back of the paper image. You may want to do a couple of test images until you get the technique down.

3. **THEN PRESS PAPER** with a wood craft stick with medium pressure. You need enough pressure to transfer the ink but not enough to rip the paper or cause the ink to be blotchy.

4. **LET DRY. ONCE** it has dried overnight, the product can be heat set to make it more durable.

5. **USE A PERMANENT** brown ink pad to rub along the edges of the bag to make the bag look old. Concentrate on edges that might become worn.

Tip

If you aren't comfortable doing a solvent transfer, use a trace and transfer method and paint the text on with black acrylic paint.

FA LA LA
BURLAP BANNER

I LOVE A GOOD BURLAP BANNER. What more is there to say? I've seen many different kinds of burlap banners and I wanted to make one that would be easy to make and cute to display for the holidays! Using the template provided on the CD and precut stencils, this is a great 20-minute project, and this banner can be customized to read any holiday message you like!

Gather

Approximately 2 yards burlap
(Depending on how big you cut your flag, this will make about 10 flags per yard.)

4-inch letter stencils

Stencil brush

Black acrylic paint

Hot glue and glue gun

Garden twine

21

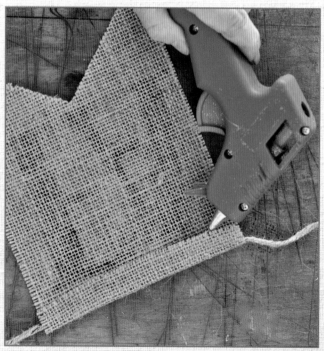

1. **FIRST DETERMINE** what your holiday message is going to be and how many banner flags you need for it. Cut banner pieces using the template provided. The burlap may unravel slightly at the edge, but that's okay. Cut as many banner flags as needed for your lettered message.

2. **WITH THE LETTER** stencil and black paint, stencil the letters on using the acrylic paint.

3. **USE HOT GLUE** to glue the banners onto the twine. It helps to precut the twine and lay out your flags for proper spacing before gluing. If you want the flags to be movable, make sure to only glue the banner to itself so it has freedom to slide along the twine.

4. **TIE A LOOP** in each end to hang.

Tip

This is actually a very versatile project and the banner can be modified to be used year-round for any occasion!

23

CHAPTER 3

❄

BY THE FIRESIDE

25

POM-POM HOLIDAY TREES

POM-POMS ALWAYS REMIND me of my childhood. There is just something about them that screams fun. I really love that they are so versatile, and I love the contrast of the white pom-poms with the prettiness of the silver tones of the different jingle bells.

Gather

Cardboard cones of various sizes

White pom-poms of various sizes—each tree takes about 250 pom-poms (I used larger pom-poms for the larger trees and the smaller ones for the smallest.)

Jingle bells in various sizes—each tree takes about 40-50 jingle bells

Super tacky white craft glue

White acrylic craft paint

1. **PAINT THE CONES** with white craft paint and let dry. This way if the pom-poms don't cover the base all of the way, the cardboard won't show through.

2. **START GLUING THE** white pom-poms on the base, working your way around it. I found it's easiest to squeeze the glue out on a plate in a glob and dip each pom-pom in the glue.

3. **AS YOU WORK** your way up the cone, leave small spaces to place your jingle bells later.

4. **ONCE YOUR POM-POMS** have dried, you can add the jingle bells. Dip the base in white craft glue and press firmly to the tree between the pom-poms. It helps to twist them a little when pressing firmly to work them between the pom-poms.

IF THE jingle bells are too heavy for super tacky white craft glue, try using a hot glue gun instead.

Tip

If you can't find cardboard cones, try using kids' party hats or making cones out of cereal boxes and masking tape.

TRY USING red and white pom-poms and gluing them in a spiral pattern for a peppermint twist!

BY THE FIRESIDE

UPHOLSTERY WEBBING
RUSTIC RED WREATH

I HAVE TO ADMIT, I ADORE JUTE upholstery webbing. It's like a piece of furniture's best-kept secret, tucked underneath all of that stuffing and fabric. It's almost like a treasure that for years was behind the scenes. I've used it for many projects and I love the idea of making a wreath out of it! The red is fun, but it also comes in many other colors, such as blue stripe or green stripe, and, in most cases, costs under 2 dollars a yard at the fabric store.

Gather

A 9-inch cardboard/chipboard wreath form

Approx. 10½ yards upholstery webbing cut as follows:

Nine 13-inch pieces

Nine 12-inch pieces

Ten 8-inch pieces

Low melt/temp hot glue sticks and glue gun

1 yard burlap ribbon

1 yard burlap ribbon with lace or ribbon of choice

Wreath hanger

31

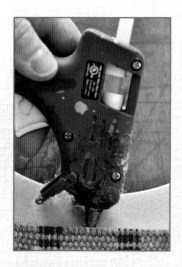
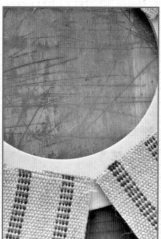

1. **START WITH THE** 13-inch pieces. Glue the first piece to the wreath form halfway between the two edges. Double the strip over and glue both pieces together, making a tab and making sure the backs are glued down to the board. Continue all the way around, making tabs with the edges touching.

2. **ONCE THE FIRST** layer is glued, start with the second layer of 12-inch pieces, making tabs and overlapping them with the first layer, but glue them at the edge of the form. It's fine if the pieces overlap slightly at their edges. Continue all the way around until you complete the second layer. Remember to glue the backs to the tabs behind them, but don't glue each tab to itself.

3. **PRETRIM THE ENDS** of the third-layer pieces by curving them in slightly so they follow the edge of the wreath form when you glue them on. They don't need to be perfect; they will be covered later. Make the third layer with the 8-inch pieces the same way the first two were made, overlapping slightly at the edges to fit all of the pieces.

4. **ONCE THE THIRD** layer is glued on, use the 1 yard of burlap ribbon and hot glue it to the edge of the inside of the wreath, trimming any excess. This will cover any messy or uneven edges. Make sure to leave enough to glue around the backside as well.

5. **FLIP THE WREATH** over and glue the burlap ribbon all around the backside. Finish with a burlap lace bow and a drop of hot glue to place it in the front and add a hanger of choice to the back and hang!

CAUTION! Burlap is a very open woven material and it is very easy to have hot glue seep through when gluing and get burned. Always use caution when applying a piece.

Tip

Use a cardboard cake round with the center cut out if you can't find a cardboard wreath form.

YOU CAN make tabs out of almost any material to make this wreath. Try cotton duck, printed cotton, or even flannel. Be careful not to use any flammable materials with the hot glue gun as they can melt or catch fire and cause burns.

FESTIVE FIREPLACE

A FIREPLACE CAN ADD WARMTH and coziness to a home. And whether it's a real working fireplace or just a faux mantel, it lends lots of opportunities for decorating! Decorating doesn't have to be expensive or involved; it can be a matter of "shopping your own home" for things you already have (or "shopping your neighbor's home" if you know them well enough!).

WITH THIS fireplace, it was a matter of pulling things from around the house and adding greenery.

MERCURY GLASS and clear candleholders, ornaments, and candles make up a festive display.

A SIMPLE WREATH holds a Celtic drum with a nod to the homeowner's heritage and personalizes the display.

35

SPARKLY DOILY BANNER

THE ONE THING I HAVE A LOT of, but I never know what to do with, is doilies. I know they are made by machine now, but I think about all of the hours my grandmother spent tatting out these intricate tiny snowflakes from fine cotton thread and I just sit in awe. This banner reminds me of her and her dedication to doing something she loved to make something pretty. Many of my doilies are a mixture of vintage and old, and I love giving them new life with this project.

Gather

Cotton doilies of various sizes

White craft glue

Paintbrush

Super fine crystal glitter

Twine or yarn to hang doilies

1. "PAINT" WHITE CRAFT glue onto the back side of the doily and let dry. This will help stiffen the doily.

2. FLIP OVER AND repeat the same on the front, except this time sprinkle with glitter before dry. Tap off excess glitter.

3. REPEAT FOR THE rest of the doilies and let them lie flat to dry.

4. RUN A PIECE of string or twine through each doily and hang.

CAUTION! If you are going to use this as mantel decor, make sure it is on a faux mantel or nonworking fireplace. The banner could be flammable.

Keep out of reach of children as the twine could be a strangulation hazard.

Tip

Use smaller doilies to make individual ornaments for your tree or as embellishments on gifts.

MERCURY GLASS CANDLEHOLDER

I LOVE THE LOOK OF MERCURY glass during the holidays. It has a certain sparkle with a hint of patina that makes it the perfect winter decor, and I love how it all looks lined up on a fireplace mantel even through January.

With mercury glass spray paint, it's easy to turn any piece of glass into something pretty. I used a 49-cent thrift store vase, and I added a twist by adding an image window on the front with some printable clear sticker paper and a vintage image. (Used with permission from *The Graphics Fairy*.)

I always recommend using battery-operated candles in projects like this; it's just safer and you don't have to worry if you forget to blow them out!

Gather

Mercury glass spray paint

Clear glass container

Clear printable
sticker paper

Printer

Vintage images

Card stock

BY THE FIRESIDE

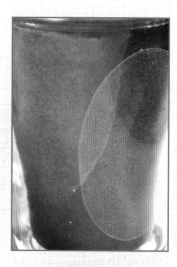

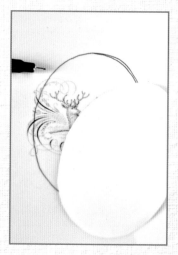

1. DECIDE WHAT SIZE and shape image window you would like. I used an oval, but you can do any shape. Trace it onto clear sticker paper and cut it out. This will be a mask to keep the glass clear while you spray.

2. CLEAN YOUR GLASS piece to remove any tags, oils, or sticky residue. Peel the back off the clear sticker paper and retain backing. Stick the clear sticker onto your glass container where you would like your image window to be. Make sure the edges are firmly stuck to the container.

3. LINE THE INTERIOR of the glass piece with card stock. Following the directions on the can, give your container several coats of mercury glass spray until you achieve the coverage you would like.

4. WHILE YOUR CONTAINER is drying, print out your image in the size needed. Print several images on one sheet at a time so you don't waste an entire sheet of sticker paper for one small image. You can use these in other projects later. Use the backing retained from the clear sticker to trace your shape. Cut out just to the inside of your tracing lines.

5. ONCE YOUR CONTAINER is dry, carefully peel off the clear sticker. Remove any sticker residue. You are ready to add your own custom-printed image. Carefully remove the backing and place your sticker on the clear window space. Press the sticker firmly to remove any air bubbles.

6. USE A BATTERY-OPERATED candle for best results.

Tip

If you don't want to use your printer, you can also stamp on your sticker paper with permanent ink.

YOU CAN ALSO monogram these or add a photo for a winter wedding centerpiece or shower!

USE GOLD or colored spray paint for a different look or season.

BY THE FIRESIDE

43

VINTAGE PICTURE BEAD GARLAND

I SOMETIMES LIKE TO MAKE home decor that can carry through the holiday season and not have to come down the minute I rip the Christmas decorations down. Or, I like to have something else that isn't too springy to go up and replace the Christmas decor.

This project has a fun vibe and is a cute winter garland to hang on your stairway or the mantel of your unlit fireplace.

I took a photo of a vintage thrift store picture, printed it with my computer, and glued it on cardboard stars. The bead garland is just wooden beads from the craft store. It's nice because they come already stained and finished, so it's just a matter of stringing them on twine and marrying the two projects for a funky winter garland.

Gather

Wooden beads of various sizes (This 6-foot garland took about 85)

Garden twine

Lightweight cardboard

Photo of a vintage painting printed out on white card stock

Glue stick

Hot glue and glue gun

1. **FOR A 6-FOOT** garland, use a piece of twine approximately 8 feet long. Tie a bead at the far end and start stringing beads. About every 3rd or 4th bead, tie a knot in the twine. These knots will be where you glue your stars. When you reach the length you desire, tie a bead off at the end.

2. **FOR THE STARS,** print a vintage picture on card stock. Trace and cut star shapes out of cardboard. Glue stars to the backside of the print with the glue stick.

3. **CUT THE STARS** out.

4. **HOT GLUE THE** stars at various points where the knots are.

CAUTION! Keep out of reach of children. The garland could be a choking or strangulation hazard.

Tip

Use family photos instead of vintage paintings.

ADD GLITTER to the star edges to bling it up a little for the holidays.

MAKE A slightly longer one and make the stars into an Advent calendar.

CHAPTER 4

MERRY AND BRIGHT

49

SNOWBALL JINGLE BELLS

THESE FUN ORNAMENTS ARE easy to make, fun for kids and grown ups alike, and add a bit of sparkle to the tree at the same time. Even when there aren't snowballs outside, there will be in the house!

Gather

Large jingle bells

Cotton balls

White acrylic craft paint

White tacky craft glue

Dimensional snow medium

White or clear glitter

Sparkly pipe cleaner

51

1. **USE A COTTON** ball to pat white paint onto the jingle bell. Patting with a cotton ball will give it a more snowy base look. A paint brush can be used but will leave a streaky appearance. Use 1 coat for a more rustic look. To completely cover a dark or silver jingle bell, it may take up to 3 coats, letting dry between each application.

2. **ONCE ACRYLIC PAINT** is dry, apply dimensional snow medium. It really works best if you mush it on with your fingers. If it doesn't seem to be sticking well enough, use a brush to coat the jingle bell first in a white tacky craft glue. Multiple layers of dimensional snow medium can be used for a thicker coating but must dry completely between coats to keep from cracking or lifting.

3. **AFTER THE DIMENSIONAL** snow medium dries, brush a coat of white craft glue and sprinkle glitter on the jingle bells to get the full "snowy" effect.

4. **ONCE THE BELLS** are dried, cut a sparkly pipe cleaner with scissors to approximately 6 inches and thread through hole at the top of the jingle bell. Twist the top to make a loop.

IF YOU CAN'T FIND dimensional snow medium, you can make your own by experimenting. Try mixing either lightweight artist modeling paste and white craft paint, white craft paint and paper-based clay, or artist's stucco medium and white craft paint.

PINECONE
HEDGEHOG AND MICE ORNAMENTS

MY KIDS ARE QUITE THE AVID collectors. A few hours in the yard can result in stray sticks, rocks, and pinecones. They seem to float around the house and turn up in unexpected places, such as in drawers, under beds, and occasionally in the dryer. Couple that with a love of a good pinecone/clay craft and these cute little holiday hedgehogs and mice are born.

Gather

An air-dry or paper-based clay

Pinecones

Hot glue and glue gun

White craft paint

Black craft paint

Gold craft paint

Gold cord

1. **REMOVE THE SMALLEST** first ⅓rd of the pine-cones scales (those are the hard parts that make the pine cone look like a pine cone). It may be possible to do it with kitchen shears, or by twisting the scales off. Wear eye protection in case a scale chips off while cutting. Keep a few same-sized scales on the side for the ears to add later.

2. **ONCE THE SCALES** are off, take a piece of clay approximately the size of a small ping-pong ball (about 1–1⅛ inches) and roll into a ball shape. Once you have a ball shape, roll one end only to become a cone.

3. **FLATTEN AND FLAIR** the edge of the ball end and push the clay over the de-scaled pinecone end. The difference between the mouse and hedgehog ornament are the snout sizes. I use twice as much clay for the mouse. Once the clay is securely on the pinecone, reshape the nose as needed (it's a cute little upturned point) and use 2 of the pinecone scales as ears by pushing them into the clay about halfway up the face.

4. **ONCE THE CLAY** is dry, paint the face with white or cream paint. Also paint white and gold onto the top of the scales. Use a skewer or the end of a small paintbrush to dot 2 eyes in black craft paint, and dip the nose in a small bit of gold paint.

5. **USE HOT GLUE** to add a gold cord as a hanger. If you have a heavier clay, make sure it is positioned a little bit closer to the front.

Tip

Paper-based clay might be heavier than an air-dry clay, so make sure to place the hanger closer to the top of the head.

YARN TASSEL GARLAND

I COULD HOARD YARN IF GIVEN the opportunity. I learned to crochet from my Polish grandmother at 9 and developed a love for the texture and feel of yarn at a very young age. We never have to buy hats because the minute the weather has a nip in the air, I crave yarn and whip out my crochet hook and get to work! This leads to a very large collection of leftovers. I love this garland because it makes use of all the extra bits and pieces of yarn from projects (and hats!).

Gather

Chunky yarn in various colors (this garland has 5)

A 9-foot piece of yarn from any of the colors

Cardboard square approx. 5 × 5 inches

Scissors

12.5-cm/5-inch weaving needle

1. **WRAP THE CHUNKY** yarn around the cardboard square approximately 20 times.

2. **CUT THE YARN** at the base straight across, keeping the yarn together.

3. **CAREFULLY PULL THE** yarn off, keeping it flat. Twist the yarn in the middle until it twists in on itself.

4. **TIE AND KNOT** an approximately 5-inch piece of matching yarn around the top, making a little "head" for the tassel.

5. **TRIM THE TASSEL** base with scissors, making the yarn-ends even. Continue making tassels. This garland has 16 tassels.

6. **WITH THE WEAVING** needle threaded with a contrasting color, "sew" the 9-foot piece of yarn through the top of a tassel.

7. **TIE A KNOT** as you go along. Add the next tassel and do the same. It might be a little difficult to tie the first few on because of the extra length of yarn, but it gets easier as the piece gets shorter.

8. **TIE LOOPS IN** the end to hang.

Tip

You can make the tassels longer or shorter by making the cardboard square longer or shorter.

TRY A really cool textured yarn for a different look.

MAKE individual tassels to tie on packages and gifts

RUBBER STAMP ORNAMENTS

I'VE QUITE A COLLECTION OF those stamps from the dollar bin. I can't possibly use them all, so I thought it would be cute to turn them into ornaments.

Gather

Dollar bin stamps
(It works best with stamps with bold images and no words or text.)

Holiday message stamp

White spray paint

White craft glue

Foam craft brush

Ultrafine glitter in choice of colors

Paper plate

Hot glue

5-inch length of ribbon

63

1. **REMOVE ANY LOOSE** stickers or labels. Spray paint the entire stamp, top and bottom, until it's completely white. Let dry.

2. **USE PERMANENT INK** to stamp a holiday message on the back of the blank stamp area.

3. **STAMP THE RAISED** rubber image part of the painted stamp onto a permanent ink color that is similar to the glitter color.

4. **ONCE IT'S DRY,** use a foam craft brush to lightly brush glue onto the raised stamp area, taking care not to glob it on and get it in any of the cracks.

5. **SPRINKLE GLITTER ONTO** a paper plate in a light layer and stamp the wet glue area into the glitter to over the image. Let dry.

6. **ONCE IT'S DRY,** tie the ribbon with a loop in the center about 1 inch long. Hot glue the loose part of the ribbon around the edges of the stamp to make a hanger.

Tip

Experiment with different paint color and glitter color combinations.

MERRY AND BRIGHT

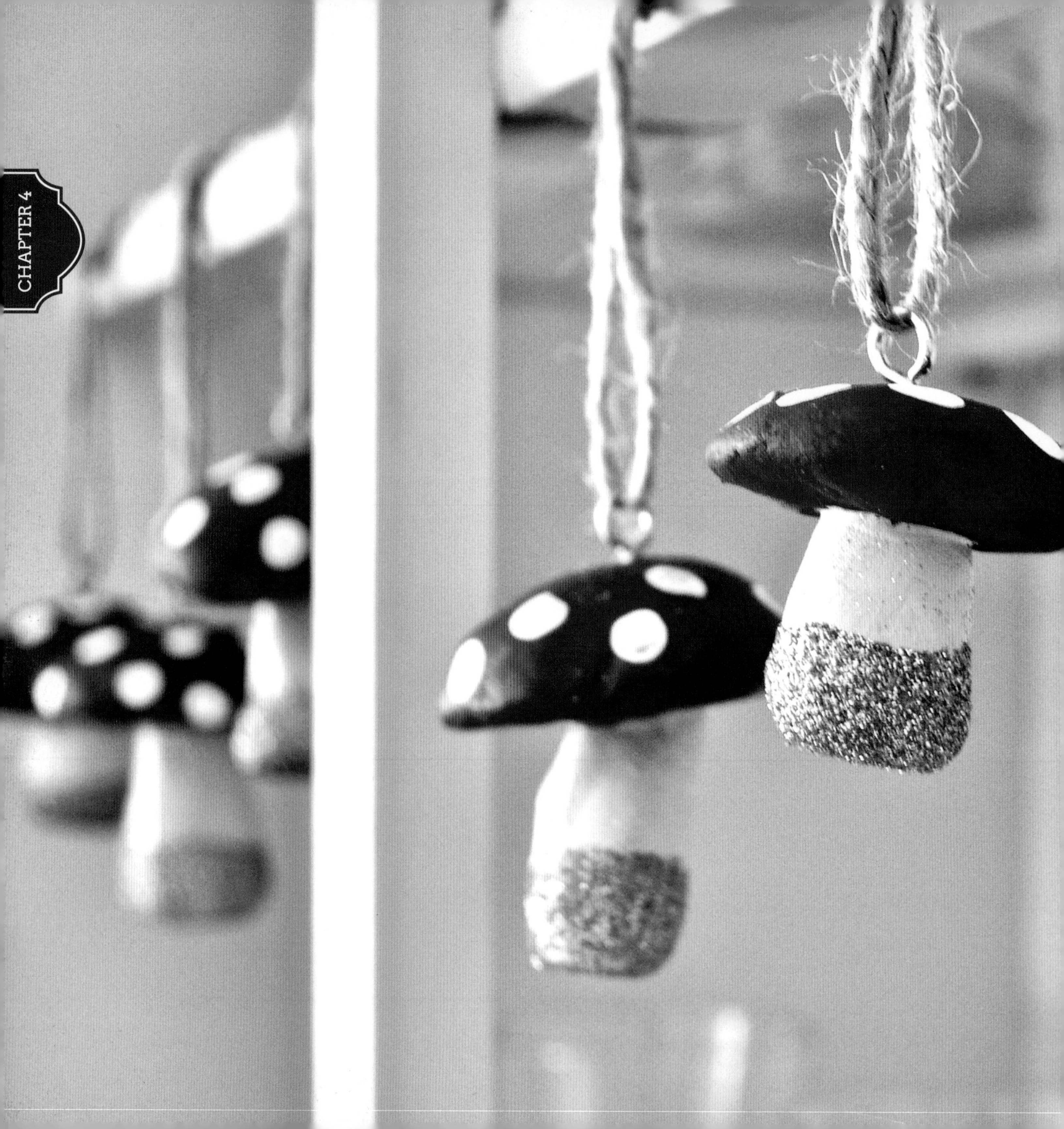

HOLIDAY TOADSTOOL ORNAMENTS

I LOVE THE IDEA OF SWEET little mushroom ornaments for Christmas. These are fun fungi to make and decorate with, and they add a nice pop of color to the green tree. I was curious why we even use fungus in decorating, and after web searching, I found that the red and white dotted mushrooms we associate with Christmas actually grow under pine trees as their natural habitat. In some cultures they are considered good luck, and I also found out they are super-poisonous too.

I prefer the much safer route by making mine out of clay. These also have a little glitter at the bottom to add a nice bit of sparkle.

Gather

Paper-based
or air-dry clay

White tacky craft glue

Small screw-type
eye hooks

Red, white, and cream
acrylic craft paint

Paintbrushes

Super fine glitter

Twine

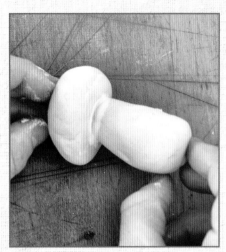

1. **MAKE TWO BALLS** out of clay, approximately the size of a ping-pong ball. Roll one ball into a cylinder shape, letting one end taper a bit more than the other. The second ball flatten the bottom but leave the top rounded. This will be your cap and base. Now is a good time to also use your thumb and carefully make a small indentation in the underside of the flat part of the mushroom cap, flip it back over, and while still wet, stick the screw eye in.

2. **SMALL CRACKS MAY** appear while drying. Either use more clay to smooth them out, or just paint them over. Once dry, use white craft glue to glue the cap to the base. Let dry.

3. **PAINT THE CAP** red and the base cream. After dry, use an unused pencil eraser to make the dots on the cap with white craft paint. Let dry.

4. **ONCE DRY, USE** a paintbrush and white tacky glue to paint a line around the bottom of the mushroom base and the rest of the bottom.

5. **SPRINKLE FINE GLITTER** over the top, turning as you go to make sure the glue-painted areas are completely covered.

6. **ADD TWINE THROUGH** the loop in the eye hook and hang! Experiment in making them all different sizes.

THESE CAN ALSO be used as fun place card holders. Instead of adding an eye hook at the top, when you are molding the cap, make a indentation to hold a name card or photo by gently pushing in with a playing or business card, and make sure the bottom of the stem is flat so it will stand on its own.

MERRY AND BRIGHT

GRAIN SACK–INSPIRED PAPER CHAIN

RED-STRIPED GRAIN SACKS ARE the inspiration behind this project. It's super easy, and a fun way to spend a snowy afternoon. Use the printables (in red or aqua) provided to make the basis for the chain and start cutting!

Gather

Plain white paper

Printer

Glue stick

Scissors

Ruler

1. **PRINT THE PRINTABLE** provided onto plain white paper. You want to print so the stripes go the long way on the paper. 4 ordinary-sized sheets of printer paper will make a 4-foot chain.

2. **CUT THE PRINTED** paper into strips, 1½ inches wide and 9 inches long. You should get 5 strips per page.

3. **USING THE GLUE** stick, apply glue to a portion of the top side of one of the strip-ends and, making a loop, glue the top side to the bottom side at the opposite end overlapping.

4. **FOR THE SECOND** chain, apply the glue, loop it through the first chain, and glue the ends as in the previous step.

5. **CONTINUE DOWN THE** chain until you reach the desired length.

Tip

You can also use scrapbook paper for this project.

THIS PRINTABLE is also used in the Decoupaged Grain Sack–Inspired Picture Frame (p. 133), but you can also print this on card stock and use a tag puncher to make gift tags.

DIFFERENT PRINTERS and computers read color differently. If the printable isn't printing out the correct color, you may need to tweak it a little bit in your photo program.

CHAPTER 5

HOLLY AND IVY

75

NATURAL HOME TOUCHES

BOXWOOD IS A GREAT alternative for those allergic to pine at the holidays. It can be found either fresh or preserved. While preserved boxwood wreaths and swags can be pricey, they can also last for years to come with careful storage. Fresh boxwood is much more affordable and can even be grown in many places in the United States, but it only makes it about one holiday season before the small yet brittle leaves break off as the plant dries out.

FRESH BOXWOOD stands in for Santa's "hair" in these vintage holiday mugs.

HOLLY AND IVY

SMALL SPRIGS in vintage bottles add a nice bit of greenery through winter.

78

VINTAGE SILVER chafing dish lids hung on the wall for a touch of silver are embellished with small leftover pieces of boxwood.

THIN BRANCHES wired together and hung around chandelier arms (away from any lighting or electrical elements), along with vintage ornaments, add a pretty and festive touch.

A SMALL POSY of boxwood embellishes vintage books.

79

RUSTIC
HOME TOUCHES

USING NATURAL ELEMENTS TO decorate for the holidays is as easy as looking around to see what you already have. This home takes on a cozy, lodge-like feel even though tucked in a busy Chicago suburb.

BIRCH LOGS and greenery collected from nearby are a great natural element and texture to add and many times have the benefit of being free. Even though the room is more on the masculine side, decorative mercury glass ornaments add a nice touch of sparkle.

POPS OF RED help add a bit of welcome color to an otherwise neutral palette. The wreath with berries on the base of the trophy buck adds that pop of color to the neutral stone fireplace and adds to the rustic quality of the room. A black vintage trunk serves as a coffee table without blocking the view to the fireplace.

THE TREE decor is kept more on the neutral side; extra antlers are tucked in the tree boughs among found branches from the yard and berry clusters. A piece of industrial metal art tucked behind the tree adds a nice touch of color and a bit of surprise to the room.

A VINTAGE berry basket of mixed pinecones gets an added pop of winter from flocking spray.

BIRCH-WRAPPED CANDLES

I LOVE THE LOOK OF BIRCH AT the holidays. It reminds me of snow-topped mountains and the rustic nature of winter. This project pairs well with battery-operated or "flameless" candles for a pretty and natural look.

Gather

Long birch sheets, approx. 5 x 11 inches each, long enough to wrap around the candles with some overlap

Garden twine

Fresh or faux greenery

Battery-operated candles

85

1. **WRAP BIRCH SHEETS** around battery-operated candles.

2. **TIE WITH TWINE.** I like to loop it 5 or 6 times for a rustic look.

3. **IF YOU ARE** buying bulk pieces of birch, you might have to go through and find the thinner pieces that bend easily. For slightly thicker pieces, soak the birch strips in hot water for about 5 minutes to make them flexible. Roll and tie them in a loose roll while still wet. Once they are dry, you can put them around the candle.

4. **ADD GREENERY OR** berries tucked in the twine for a more holiday feel. Remove the greenery to keep out year-round.

GLITTERY MOSS STARS

I LOVE DECORATING ALL YEAR with natural elements, but I think they are even more beautiful with the sparkle of the holidays. Moss has such a pretty textural element, and the combination of the glitter and gold wire against the green gives a very pretty contrast. These would be great for ornaments or gift embellishments, or even in a floral display. The best part is, they aren't super expensive to make. I just used some old shipping boxes I had in the garage for the star base.

Gather

Sheet moss

Reindeer moss

Cardboard

White craft glue

Twine

22 gauge gold wire

Glitter

1. **CUT STARS OF** desired size out of cardboard. Use craft glue to adhere sheet moss to one side and trim around star shape. Then adhere sheet moss to second side.

2. **WHILE THE GLUE** is still wet, add the twine ends under the moss with glue to form a loop to hang the star by and let dry. Glue reindeer moss to both sides of star.

3. **WRAP STAR IN GOLD** wire going around several times, tucking the ends under when finished.

4. **BRUSH THE MOSS** star with white craft glue and liberally apply glitter. Let dry.

5. **HANG INDIVIDUALLY AS** decorations or string together as a garland.

Tip

If you can't find sheet moss, you can also use regular craft moss.

GOLD-COLORED wire will probably be in the jewelry aisle, and moss will be in the floral aisle.

HOLLY AND IVY

GLITTERY SCATTER ACORNS

ADD A LITTLE GLAM TO YOUR decorations with these glittery scatter acorns. There is something about their sweet little tops. They remind me of tiny berets. I wanted to make some glittery acorns for a pretty accent that I could reuse year after year. Real acorns are pretty on their own, but real acorns may have grubs inside and need to be baked in an oven to kill them (it's not very festive to find those in a bowl), and the nut part of the acorn can also go rancid after time and attract mice. The best option is to just gather the empty tops after the squirrels have taken their share and substitute the nut part for little Styrofoam balls found in the dried floral supply aisle.

Gather

Empty acorn tops

Small Styrofoam balls, approx. $\frac{1}{4}$- to $\frac{1}{2}$-inch depending on the size of your caps

White craft glue

Brush

Glitter of choice (ultrafine glitter works best)

Plastic square or wax paper to dry on

1. **GLUE STYROFOAM BALLS** and acorn tops together with a generous dollop of white craft glue. Let dry.

2. **USE BRUSH TO** coat entire outside of acorns with glue.

3. **APPLY GLITTER TO** acorns and set on a piece of plastic or wax paper to dry.

Tip

If you can't find the right size Styrofoam balls for bases, use air-dry clay to sculpt acorn bottoms.

ULTRAFINE glitter works best, but you can use any glitter you have.

ADD SMALL screw eyes in the tops and make a glittery acorn garland.

CHAPTER 6

❄

UNDER THE
TREE

97

HANDSTAMPED WASHI-INSPIRED DIY GIFT WRAP TAPE

I LOVE WASHI TAPE. WASHI TAPE is a decorated paper tape that originated in Japan. It goes beyond the boring old beige of masking tape and has beautiful colors and patterns! It can be used for everything from decorating envelopes and packages to all kinds of craft projects. While there are a ton of options to choose from, I always find there's a color pattern/combination I want that I just can't find. Hence, DIY washi tape!

Gather

Drafting tape
(You can find it at art and hobby stores. It looks like masking tape, but it's thinner and more flexible.)

8 x 11 plastic craft sheet

Acrylic paint, color of choice

Cotton balls

Stamps

Permanent ink

Paintbrush

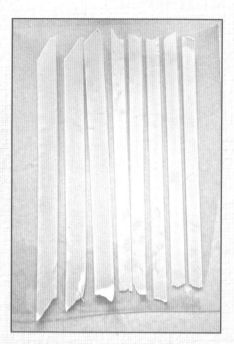

1. **TEAR STRIPS OF** the drafting tape and lay them out on the plastic sheet.

2. **PAINT EACH STRIP** with the acrylic craft paint of choice.

3. **REMOVE EXCESS PAINT** with a cotton ball.

4. **ONCE THE PAINT** is dry, use the permanent ink to stamp a pattern on to the tape.

5. **ONCE IT IS** dry, carefully peel the tape off the plastic sheet. Use the tape to decorate!

Christmas

CARVE YOUR OWN STAMPS FOR HAND-PRINTED TAGS

LINOCUTTING IS AN OLD ART which involves carving a reverse image onto a hard linoleum sheet with a V-shaped razor-sharp cutter and printing the relief of the carved-out image. I first learned to linocut in 8th grade. Somehow, our hippy art teacher thought it was an amazing idea to let a bunch of teenagers work with really sharp tools on a hard-to-cut surface. She would yell out "Hands behind your tool!" and someone would always slip while pushing super hard and end up in the emergency room with a V-shaped stitch in their hand.

The reindeer and faux bois images provided are fun stamps to make and easy to use. I use both stamp ink and block printing ink with mine. Luckily, linocutting has come a long way, and you can buy soft pink blocks that are really easy to carve and print with, but the same advice holds true as it did some . . . umm . . . 30 years ago. "Hands behind your tool!"

Gather

2 pink 6 x 12 linocut
speedy carve blocks

1 linocutting set
with gouges (blades)
(small *V* and large *U*)

Images

Transfer paper

Pen

Stamp ink
or block printing ink

Paper or tag to print onto

103

1. **PRINT YOUR IMAGE** in reverse of the way you want your stamp to print. This deer was printed at 3 inches by 4 inches so it would fit on the pictured tag. Reduce or enlarge as needed to fit what you are printing onto. Place your lino block on a very flat and firm surface where it can't slip.

2. **PLACE YOUR TRANSFER** paper down and then your image on top in the very center of the 6 x 12 block. Use a pen to trace around the outline of your image to transfer the image to the block.

3. **ONCE THE IMAGE** is transferred, you are ready to carve. Leave the block at its full size; you can trim it later. Leaving it at its full size gives you something to grip onto while carving. Always follow the full directions on the linocutting kit before starting, and follow all safety directions! A linocut tool is very sharp and can cause serious injury if the directions are not followed correctly.

4. **HOLDING THE STAMP** firmly and **KEEPING YOUR HAND BEHIND THE LINOCUTTER**, gently carve around the image following the outline with the small V-shaped cutting gouge. Turn the stamp as needed, always keeping any body parts behind the cutting tool and always carving away from your body. Don't carve while turning. Turn the stamp first, make sure it's firmly in place, and then carve.

5. **ONCE YOU HAVE** your image outlined, switch gouges to the large U and remove any excess pink material. When you think you have it all carved, do a test stamp and see if there are any portions that still need to be removed.

6. **ONCE YOU HAVE** it carved the way you like, you are ready to print!

Tip

You can also print with acrylic paint, but you will need to add an extender to the paint so it doesn't dry too fast.

USE SCREEN PRINTING

or fabric paint to print on fabric for tote bags, towels, and more.

UNDER THE TREE

BURLAP
FOREST ANIMAL TAGS

THIS PROJECT HAS SOME OF MY favorite things to craft with: decoupage medium, card stock, burlap, and baker's twine. I added the element of embroidery by monogramming the gift recipient's initial, but if you wanted to use these as plain gift tags, the card stock makes the back very writable. The best part of the monogramming is you don't have to buy extra embroidery floss; baker's twine is very easy to recolor with a marker color of choice. Vary your stitches to make each one a little different. I used a heavy-duty upholstery needle to sew through the layers of paper, burlap, and medium. You can use the templates provided to make forest animals, or you could use a person's silhouette too. These could also be used as ornaments or strung together as a banner.

Gather

Decoupage medium

Burlap

Natural-colored card stock

Baker's twine

Foam brushes

Marker

Scissors

Heavy-duty needle

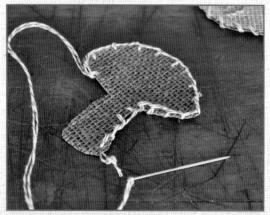

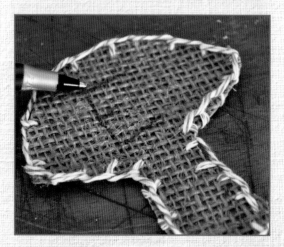

1. **BRUSH DECOUPAGE MEDIUM** onto natural-colored card stock until completely covered. Brush more decoupage medium onto burlap, thoroughly saturating the burlap. Let dry.

2. **CUT OUT TEMPLATES** and trace image onto dried burlap and card stock. Cut out traced images to just inside your tracing line. Set the card stock cutout aside for the end.

3. **USE A HEAVY-DUTY** needle threaded with doubled baker's twine to stitch around the edge of the burlap cutout in stitch of choice.

4. **YOU CAN STOP** here or continue to monogramming by tracing the initial first.

5. **STITCH THE INITIAL** onto the burlap tag, using a drop of glue when done to keep the twine from unraveling. Use the craft glue to glue the card stock cutout to the back of the monogrammed burlap.

6. **EITHER PUNCH** a hole in the top to put twine through for hanging, or sew a loop on the top of the tag.

Tip

You can also make these tags with different card stock colors or cotton fabric.

GOLD LEAF BIRCH TAGS

I LOVE GOLD LEAF. THERE'S something about it that is so satisfying. It's much simpler than it looks and has a great end result. Choose very thin birch strips for this project, since they are easier to cut with scissors.

Gather

Thin birch bark strips

Scissors

Gold leaf adhesive

Gold leaf

Pen or pencil

Small paintbrush

Large soft brush

111

1. **USE SCISSORS TO** cut the birch bark into strips 3 inches wide by 5 inches tall. Cut the top two corners off to make a tag shape and carefully bore, punch, or drill a hole through the top of the tag.

2. **DRAW A HEART** or any other shape, or even an initial, on the tag.

3. **USE A PAINTBRUSH** to paint the gold leaf adhesive to just outside of your shape so that the line doesn't show when you gold leaf the tag. Follow the directions on the bottle. Most of the time, gold leaf adhesive needs to cure for 15–30 minutes to achieve its full tackiness.

4. **ONCE THE ADHESIVE** is ready, carefully lay a paper-thin sheet of gold leaf onto the sticky area. Gold leaf is very thin and tears easily.

5. **USE A VERY** soft brush to apply pressure in a circular motion to remove any gold leafing that is not on the adhesive. If you have a spot on the tag that the leafing doesn't stick to, you can add more adhesive, let it cure again, and add more leaf.

Tip

While leafing can take a little practice, the results are worth it!

YOU CAN LEAF ornaments, picture frames, just about anything it will stick to.

CHAPTER 7

FROM THE HEART

115

JUMPING REINDEER HAND-STENCILED TEA TOWEL

THIS FUN AND EASY PROJECT makes a great gift for giving (or keeping for yourself!). It uses regular old sticky-back shelf liner for your stencil base, and you can use (your own image or) the template provided to make a bit of useful holiday cheer for your kitchen! The nice thing about reindeer is they can be out the entire winter season, so you can leave it out long after the ornaments have been packed away.

Gather

Cotton tea towel

Fabric paint color of choice

Image

Ballpoint pen

Sticky-back shelf liner

Transfer paper

Craft knife

Paintbrush or stencil pouncer

8 x 11 plastic sheet or aluminum foil

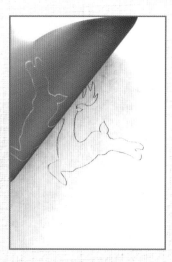

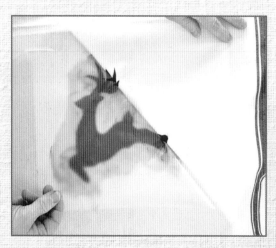

1. **LAY YOUR SHELF** liner down, paper backing-side down, liner-side up. Place your transfer paper down and your image on top of that. Press firmly with the pen and outline the image to transfer. Make an X on the area you want to cut out.

2. **PREWASH, DRY, AND** iron your towel to remove any sizing. Lay your towel flat and place a piece of white paper underneath it to catch any paint bleed through.

3. **CAREFULLY CUT YOUR** image from the shelf liner to make your stencil. Peel the paper backing off your stencil and place the image on the towel. It might help to peel and stick as you go to keep the sticky paper from rolling and sticking to itself.

4. **ONCE THE STENCIL** is adhered to the towel, press firmly, especially around the edges, to keep the paint from bleeding under. Load the brush or pouncer with paint and then off-load onto a paper towel to remove any excess. If you are using a pouncer, make sure to use a straight up and down motion.

5. **START PAINTING IN** the stencil by working inward, careful not to paint outward, which may force paint under the stencil and cause bleeding. Once the stencil is completely filled in, use a paper towel to remove any excess paint off of the stencil.

6. **LET DRY AND** remove stencil. Place stencil on a piece of firm plastic or even aluminum foil for reuse (stencil can be used 2 or 3 more times before it loses its stickiness). Set ink according to directions on bottle to make towel washable.

Sale!
SHORTY COATS
$12.88 - $15.88
FORMERLY to $29.95

COAT Sale!
$29.88
Drastic Reductions

Special!
Rain or Shine
COATS
$11.00

JOY TOTE BAG

I CAN NEVER HAVE ENOUGH tote bags. Whether it's hauling my groceries home from the store, or loading up a few to return some overdue library books, I am constantly grabbing a tote bag from the collection hanging in my hall closet. This bag adds a bit of holiday bling and can be used to deliver a gift or as the gift itself. You can add a holiday word like I did, or even do a monogram for year-round use.

Gather

1 cotton tote bag

Fabric glue or embellishment glue

Sequin trim (mine took 1½ yards)

1 pom-pom

Pencil with clean eraser

Scissors

1. IRON COTTON TOTE bag to get out any wrinkles or fold marks. You won't be able to do it once everything is adhered.

2. USE A PENCIL to lightly trace a word onto the bag.

3. PRE-LAY OUT YOUR sequin trim over the word, cutting your trim to size so when you go to lay it out, it fits perfectly and there's no hassle of cutting with the glue.

4. USE THE GLUE to trace the pencil lines. Depending on the type of glue you use, you may have to add the sequin trim as you go. (Make sure to read the instructions for proper usage.)

5. LAY OUT YOUR trim onto the glue, one letter at a time. Use a clean eraser to help push the trim into place.

6. ONCE YOUR LETTERS are outlined, glue any loose sequins around the bag randomly.

7. GLUE A POM-POM on top of the J (in this case) and let the glue dry completely before use.

FROM THE HEART

HAND-LETTERED GIFT BOTTLE LABELS

I DON'T KNOW IF IT WAS THE way I was raised or just a quirk, but I hate coming to an event or party empty-handed, even when the hostess tells me to not bring anything. A bottle of wine has always worked as a great last-minute gift for me. I always have an extra bottle lying around. Maybe wine as a gift is a throwback to growing up in the super-groovy 1970s. My mom would send us to school just before Christmas break with a bottle of wine as a teacher's gift in each of our backpacks. In fourth grade I dropped my backpack on the way to school and the bottle exploded. It soaked me, my lunch, my homework, and all of my books. And I had no gift for my teacher. I cried and cried . . . and smelled like a great party all day.

Gather

Paper

Scissors

Glue stick

Printer

1. **USE THE HAND-LETTERED** label template to make a gift a little nicer and a little more seasonal. Easily apply labels by printing them with your computer, cutting them to size, and then adhering them with a bit of tape or glue at the back.

2. **FOR NONDRINKERS,** or the chefs in your family, you can also add these labels to olive oil bottles, sparkling cider, or even balsamic vinegar. You can also print this image as a card on your computer. Simply save to your photo program or print onto card stock or craft paper, add a spring of rosemary or ribbon, and you have an easy, last-minute gift!

Notes

SILHOUETTE WRITING JOURNAL

I AM A PAPER PERSON. I LOVE paper. I love writing. I adore the sound a pencil makes when it scratches on a really good paper. I would love to get a journal as a gift any day of the week, let alone one that seems like it's a treat to open. The nice thing about this project is we are customizing a premade journal by covering it and doing a new twist on a silhouette. I used a photocopy of an old oil painting, but you can use any picture. If you don't want to use an old painting, it's as easy as taking a picture of it with your camera and printing it out on card stock. If you don't have an old oil you can use, you can also use scrapbook paper. My favorite part is the bit of sparkle at the end with a vintage brooch.

Gather

Hardcover journal
Kraft paper
Decoupage medium
Foam brushes
Craft glue
Printed picture of a vintage oil or other artwork (or scrapbook paper)
Twine
Pen or pencil
Black marker
Vintage brooch
Scissors

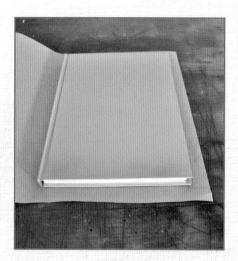

1. **CUT KRAFT PAPER** so there is a 1-inch overlap all of the way around when the journal is open. Brush decoupage medium on the front of the journal cover and then on the kraft paper. Place the two pieces together and use your hands to smooth out any globs or air bubbles.

2. **TURN THE EDGES** under at the flaps and glue down using the craft glue. After drying, trim the edges that are hanging over the top and bottom of the journal until they are flush.

3. **ONCE DRY, PRINT** out template, cut it out, and then use it to trace a silhouette image on your printed image. Cut out traced image.

4. **GLUE SILHOUETTE CUTOUT** onto cover with craft glue. With remaining printed image, cut a bookmark shape so it matches the cover.

5. **WRAP THE ENTIRE** journal in twine and add a personal touch if you like. I just added the words "notes" in black marker.

6. **ADD A VINTAGE** clip or brooch to front.

FROM THE HEART

DECOUPAGED
GRAIN SACK–INSPIRED
PICTURE FRAME

I LOVE THE LOOK OF VINTAGE grain sacks, and I love picture frames. What could be a happier marriage for a gift than combining the two? The best part is, the square frame can be purchased at your local craft store for about 2 dollars each, making it an inexpensive yet thoughtful gift.

This project is as simple as decoupaging the paper provided as a printable and trimming the excess!

Gather

Wood craft frame

Printer

Card stock

Decoupage medium

White tacky craft glue

Brush

Gray ink pad

Craft knife

Clear acrylic sealer

133

FROM THE HEART

1. **PRINT THE PRINTABLE** onto card stock. (Some computers and printers vary on how they read an image, so you may have to adjust your printer setting to get the correct color desired.)

2. **APPLY DECOUPAGE MEDIUM** to the frame front and to the entire back of the printed card stock, working quickly so the medium doesn't dry.

3. **APPLY THE CARD** stock to the frame, using your fingers to smooth and push out any air bubbles. Let dry.

4. **TRIM THE EXCESS** paper to the edges on the inside and the outside of the frame.

5. **DARKEN THE EDGES** of the frame with the gray ink pad. This will also help to disguise your edges if you happened to get any little tears in the paper while trimming. Use white craft glue to readhere any edges that curl up. To make the paper surface of the frame more durable after drying, spray with a clear acrylic sealer.

Tip

You can also use
scrapbook paper if you
don't want you use
the printable.

IF YOU FIND the ink on your
printable card stock bleeds too easily,
print out the printable and have it
color-copied at a copy store on a
printer with toner. Or you can also
use an acrylic sealer to seal the ink.

DRESS UP the edges and
corners with scrapbook paper
embellishments.

CHAPTER 8

COMFORT
AND JOY

137

CROSS-STITCH-INSPIRED MONOGRAM MUGS

I HAVE A SLIGHT OBSESSION. I love a good mug. Getting up in the morning and holding a warm cup of coffee with milk and sugar in a great mug is one of my simple joys in life. I love a good cup of hot cocoa in a great mug after a cold day in the snow too. These incredibly cute cups make a simple yet great gift on their own or filled with packets of hot cocoa mix, tea, or even cookies for your favorite mug lover.

Gather

Mugs to decorate

Permanent markers made specifically for ceramic products

Stencils in letters of choice

Painter's tape

139

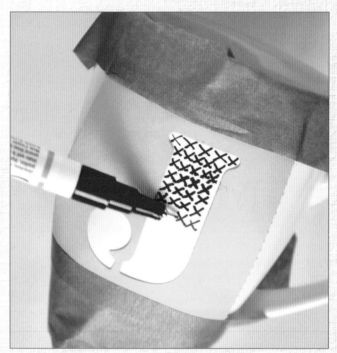

1. **CLEAN MUG TO** remove any residue off the surface that might make the marker not stick. Check the label on your marker to make sure it is food safe and nontoxic.

2. **TAPE LETTER STENCIL** to mug, making sure it's as flat as possible against the mug.

3. **START BY MAKING** small, even *X*s across the top of the letter, working down and being careful not to smudge the other *X*s.

4. **ONCE THE ENTIRE** letter is filled in, carefully remove the stencil and follow the directions for making the mug washable. When finished, fill with goodies!

GILDED
FOREST ANIMAL
PEDESTALS

I LOVE THE WAY A beautifully set table looks. That doesn't happen a lot at my house. In fact, things get broken frequently enough at our house that I stopped buying matching dishes years ago. Now I just buy plates I find pretty and slap them down as everyone plows through their meal in about 10 minutes.

The holidays are one time I like to pull out my gram's wedding china and the wine glasses from my wedding and make everything look pretty. I also think every well-dressed table has a bit of quirk to make it fun. These pedestal stands use really inexpensive materials such as glass candlesticks from the dollar store, plastic toy animals from the craft store, and gold spray paint. These can also be used for regular display as well and are meant for lighter objects. While they are fun, they aren't food safe. If you are going to use them with food, don't put any food directly on the surface; always use a real plate between so there's no contact between the food and the painted surface.

Gather

2 10-inch melamine plates

1 12-inch melamine plate

4 glass candlesticks

4 4-inch wood craft rounds

3 6-inch wood craft rounds

All-purpose heavy-duty glue (Make sure whatever glue is used can be used on plastic, wood, and glass.)

Clear acrylic sealer

Gold spray paint

Fun plastic animals, roughly 3 to 4 per base depending on size

143

1. **SPRAY THE ANIMALS** with clear acrylic sealer in a well-ventilated area and let dry so the gold paint adheres evenly.

2. **USING THE ALL-PURPOSE** glue in a well-ventilated area and following the directions, glue each candlestick bottom to its own 6-inch wood base. To make a pedestal taller, glue a 4-inch wood round to a 6-inch round, and then glue the candlestick to that. You can also flip 1 glass candlestick over on another candlestick so the candlestick bases are on the top and bottom and the mouths are glued together.

3. **FLIP A 4-INCH** wood base over and glue it to the top of a candlestick. Repeat with remaining candlesticks. Let glue dry.

4. **GLUE A MELAMINE** plate to the top of each stand and let the glue dry. Glue animals to wood base by the feet.

5. **ONCE GLUE HAS** dried, spray paint the entire stand with gold spray paint until completely covered. Let dry. Then spray with clear acrylic sealer, making sure to cover the top plate several times to prevent chipping.

Tip

It would be fun to use a different spray paint color for parties or for use in everyday decor.

MANY GLUES that bond to different surfaces are now nontoxic and not as bad as they were in the past. Hot glue can also be used on the project, but the glass bonding may not be as strong and may be more likely to fall apart.

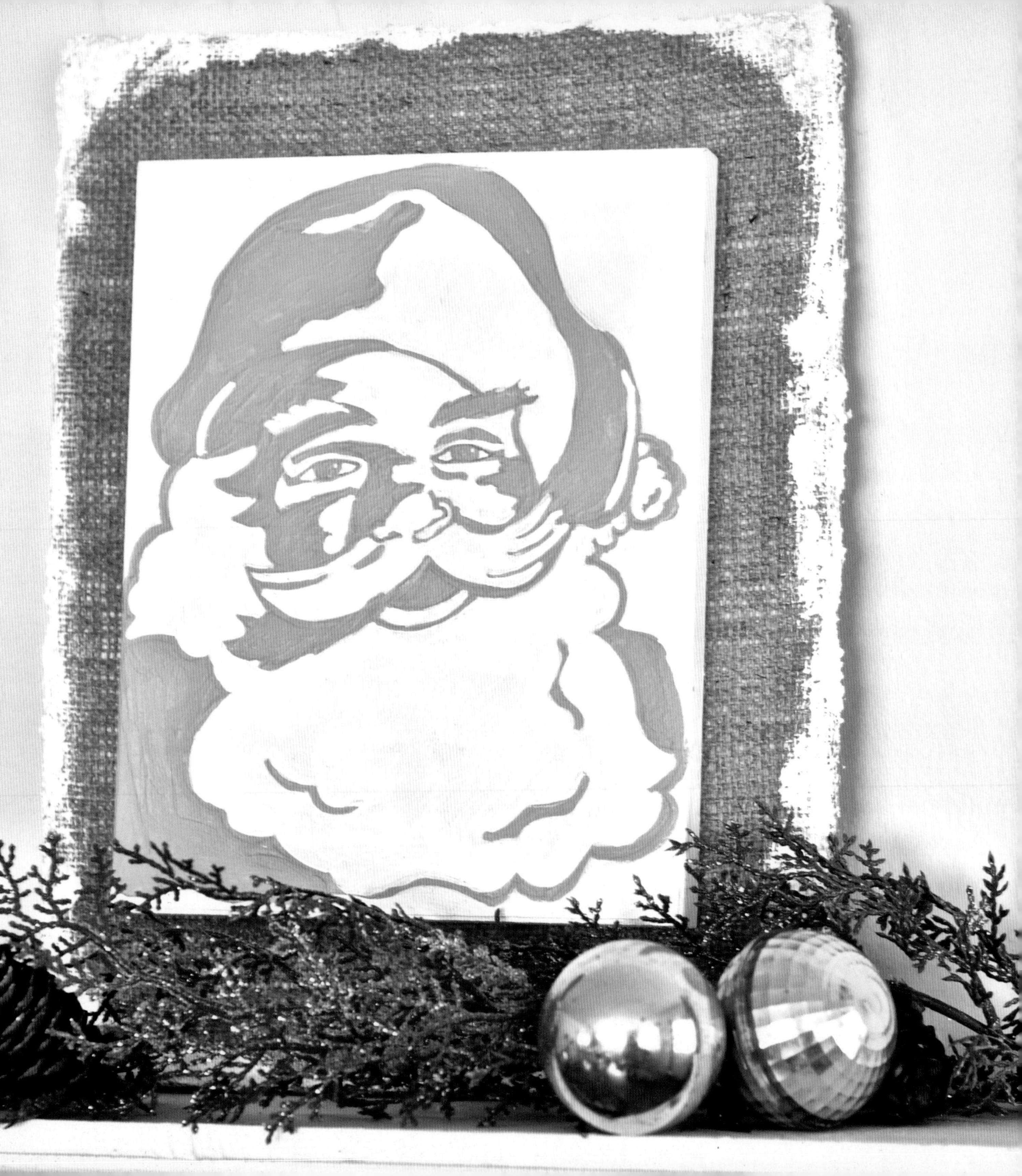

JOLLY OLD
PAINT-BY-NUMBER
SANTA PORTRAIT

SANTA IS AN ICONIC FIGURE for the holidays. Even though we shouldn't forget the true reason for the season, the magic of Santa is fun for young and old. At my house, gift lists are written in November (which makes great bribery for good behavior for the next month). As my kids have gotten older, they have heard the whisperings on the bus and the playground as to whether or not Santa is "real." My only response to them is, "If you don't believe, you don't receive." They generally stop asking after that. This project is for the artist and nonartist alike! Simply print out the provided printable paint-by-number template on your printer, glue it on a canvas, and paint in the areas marked!

Gather

1 (11 x 14) canvas
1 (8 x 10) canvas
½ yard burlap
Staple gun and staples
Santa printable provided
1 liner paintbrush
1 filler paintbrush
Matte clear acrylic
spray sealer
Dimensional snow medium
Popsicle stick
Acrylic paint in white
Acrylic paint in color
of choice
Clear glitter
White craft glue
Canvas hanger

147

1. **LAY YOUR 11 × 14 CANVAS** facedown on the burlap. Trim the burlap until it extends about 2 inches past the edge of the canvas. Pull the burlap's edges, stapling it with the staple gun around the back of the 11 x 14 canvas. If the burlap seems to unravel a bit, fold over the edge before stapling. Once the burlap is stapled to the canvas, add desired canvas hanger and put aside.

2. **PRINT OUT THE** Santa printable and trim it to an 8 x 10 size. Spray the printable with 2 coats of clear acrylic sealer (in a well-ventilated area and following the can directions!). This will help to keep the printer ink from running. Once it is dry, coat the front of the 8 x 10 canvas with white craft glue until you have an even coat. Carefully lay the Santa printable onto the canvas and smooth to remove any air bubbles. Let dry.

3. **ONCE THE PRINTABLE** is dry, you can paint! Use the liner brush to follow all of the lines, and use the filler brush to paint in any of the marked areas. Use white craft paint to go over the white areas or fix any mistakes from previous painting. Let dry.

4. **SPRAY WITH A** coat of acrylic sealer to preserve paint. Once your Santa canvas is dry, apply white craft glue to the back-side edges of the canvas and glue the Santa portrait canvas to the middle of the burlap canvas.

5. **TO GIVE A** snowy, sparkly finish to your portrait, use dimensional snow medium and apply it with a Popsicle stick (or your fingers). While the medium is still wet, sprinkle glitter on top. Let dry. If it's not sparkly enough, apply white craft glue with a brush, reapply glitter, and let dry.

Tip

After the picture is completely painted, use white craft glue to paint in the beard and add glitter to make it sparkly.

TO MAKE a bigger portrait, take it to your local printer and have them make a larger copy. They can also make engineer's prints, which can go as large as 2 feet by 3 feet.

ALWAYS USE proper safety gear when using a staple gun, especially eye protection.

Tip

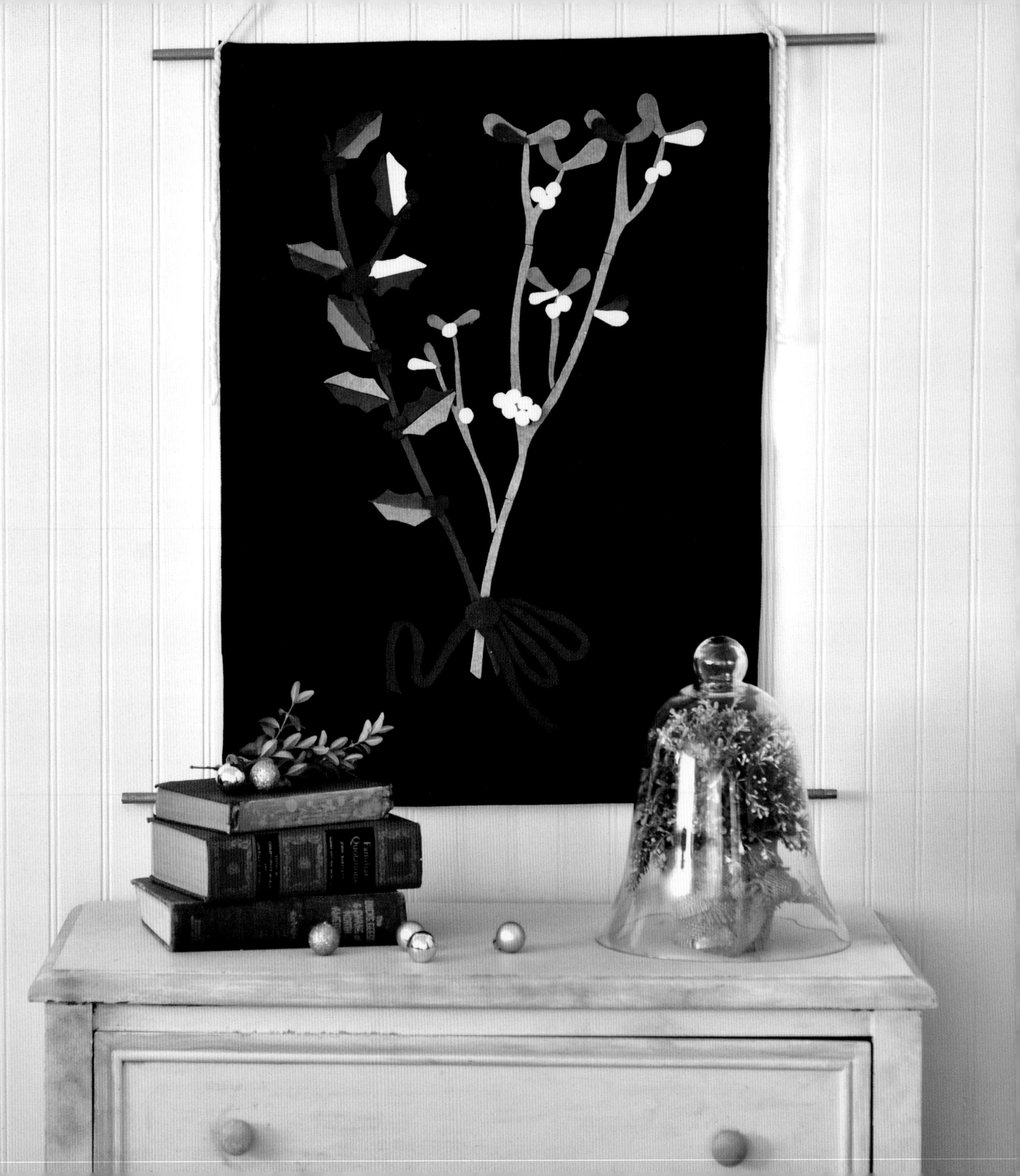

VINTAGE BOTANICAL CHART-INSPIRED FELT HANGING BANNER

I'VE ALWAYS BEEN FASCINATED with of vintage botanical illustrations. The idea that many of these were drawn and hand-colored before the benefits of a photograph to cheat from is amazing to me. The artists were able to represent all parts of a beautiful flower from a quickly wilting specimen. I thought the idea of a holiday-themed chart with holly and mistletoe would be a fun and current way to pay homage. This is a great snowy day project using the template on the CD, scissors, and a bit of glue.

Gather

1 piece of black felt, approx. 24 x 36 inches

Two 28-inch dowel rods

Gold paint

Felt glue

36 inches yarn or twine

4 (light, medium, medium-dark, dark) colors of green felt, approx. ⅛ yard each

1⅛ yards white felt

1⅛ yards off-white or cream felt

1⅛ yards red felt (for holly berries)

15 small white pom-poms (for mistletoe berries)

Template, paintbrush & straight pins

151

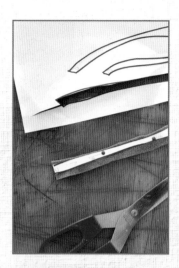

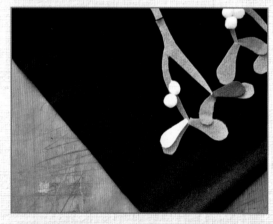

1. **PAINT YOUR DOWEL** rods with gold paint and set aside to dry.

2. **USING THE TEMPLATE** piece provided, cut out the pattern pieces, pin to the felt, and cut.

3. **TO GET TWO** holly-toned leaves, lay a lighter piece on top of the contrasting darker leaf and cut down the middle of both pieces at the same time.

4. **LAY OUT ALL** of the pieces on the black felt piece before gluing and make sure all of the pieces are there.

5. **CAREFULLY GLUE THE** felt pieces and pom-poms on, making sure not to get glue on the black felt where it will show, or it could show up as a hazy white marks. Clean up any stray glue with a lightly dampened paper towel right away.

6. **ONCE ALL OF** the pieces are glued on, let dry 24 hours.

7. **AFTER DRY, FLIP** over and turn both top and bottom edges over approximately 1 inch and glue to make a pocket for the dowel rods.

8. **ONCE THE GLUE** is dry, insert the dowel rods into the pockets and tie a piece of yarn on each end of the top dowel to hang from.

CAUTION! Keep out of reach of small children.

Tip

If a chart seems too daunting, try gluing all the elements onto a plain black pillow with fabric glue.

FELT CAN pick up little fuzzies, so use a lint roller to pick up any unwanted pieces off of the material.

IF YOU can't find the right colors of felt, you can also use flannel for a similar look.

GLITZ AND GLAM
DOILY TABLE RUNNER

WHAT MAKES THIS TABLE runner easy is the fact you start out with a premade runner. With the hard part done, it makes it fun just to dress it up a little bit. The best part of the project is that you can do any of these steps on their own without the others and it's all just as pretty and unique.

Gather

Premade table runner

Gold fabric spray paint

Temporary spray adhesive

Paper doilies

Fabric embellishment glue

Gold fabric paint

Sparkly gems or sequins

Round foam pouncer
approx. 1 inch

Paper plate for paint

155

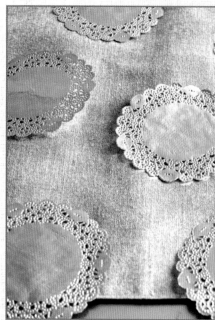

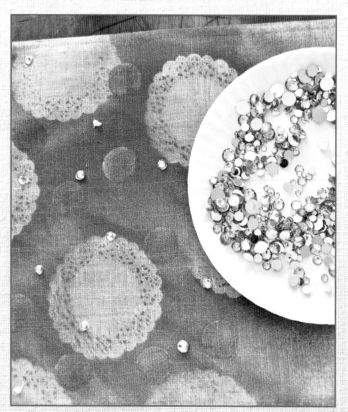

1. **SPRAY THE BACKS** of the doilies with temporary spray adhesive. Lay doilies in a random pattern on the runner and press the doilies onto it.

2. **IN A WELL-VENTILATED** area, spray the runner and doilies with the fabric spray paint. Let dry and remove the doilies.

3. **ONCE DRY, PUT** gold fabric paint on the paper plate and load the pouncer with paint. Press circles onto the runner in a random pattern. Let dry.

4. **USE THE EMBELLISHMENT** glue to glue the sparkly gems randomly to the runner. Let dry.

Tip

This table runner will
be spot clean only.

PAPER TOY
ANIMAL-INSPIRED NAPKIN RINGS

BACK IN THE EARLY 1900S the official publisher of Queen Victoria began producing easily affordable mechanical paper toys. Something about these has always interested me. They were so simple. And although they were made for children the artwork on them was so detailed and intricate. I was inspired to take that concept and make these fun napkin rings. Made with vintage images used with permission (for personal use) from *The Graphics Fairy* (www.thegraphicsfairy.com) and scrapbooking brads, these would also be fun to use as gift tags, ornaments, party favors, a fun rainy day craft, or hang tags year-round.

Gather

Heavy card stock

Printer

Scrapbooking brads

Hole punch

Scissors

Twine

Templates

1. **ON CARD STOCK,** print the animal images from the templates provided, or visit thegraphicsfairy.com for a selection of even more images. If you are using your own images, make sure to print 2 of the same images at the same size.

2. **CUT OUT ONE** image completely.

3. **ON THE SECOND** image, only cut out the parts you want to be moveable. Remove the paper parts you are replacing them with on the first image.

4. **LAY OUT YOUR** animal and use a hole punch to make the hole for the brad to be inserted into. Holding the 2 pieces you want to join together while punching them ensures the holes will line up.

5. **PUT THE BRAD** through the prepunched holes.

6. **PUNCH A HOLE** in the top and thread twine or string through the hole to hang, or wrap twine around a napkin and tie.

Tip

The size brad you use
will determine what size
hole punch to use.

CHAPTER 8

COMFORT AND JOY

CHAPTER 9

❄

THE WELL-DRESSED HOLIDAY HOME

163

EVERY YEAR at the beginning of December, a few friends and I buy tickets to see the homes in the annual neighborhood housewalk. We all pile in one car, cocoas and lattes in hand, and follow the map around town. We drive from house to house, peeking at all of the amazing decorating and holiday ideas. It is just the thing I need to get into the holiday season. I love that I get to peek into someone else's holiday decor and see all of the different ways people decorate; it definitely feeds my nosey side!

I enjoyed attending the home tours so much, it motivated me to start my own free Holiday Housewalk on my blog years ago. I thought it would be something my reader's would love to see without the 50-dollar price tag. Every year, it's become just a little bit bigger and more amazing. Having grown to over 30 homes, it's a weeklong event of holiday wonderfulness where blog readers can "walk" from house to house and never leave their own living room.

The thing I love most about it is even though many of us are attracted to some of the same things and styles, everyone's house is decorated differently. Some people like to go all out and glitter everything in sight, while other people love to keep it minimal and just add little, simple touches to their everyday spaces. That's the best thing about the holidays: they come in all shapes, colors, and sizes. There's no wrong way to decorate. It's about what you love.

I think sometimes we look at other people's "perfect" homes online or in magazines and it can make us feel a little bad about our own space because, for whatever reason, we just haven't had the chance to do what we've wanted to do to our own homes.

Things are not always what they seem.

Blog and magazine life are not real life. I know before I show a part of my home online, just like when I have a big party, I clean like crazy before I take the pictures. Sometimes when I can't, I shove the junk out of the area where the picture is going to be taken and hope I've moved it far enough out of frame. Many times I have to edit out something that didn't quite make it out of the picture (like kids toys and backpacks), or one side of the room looks great, and the other side I am not photographing looks like a tornado came through, with glitter and burlap shreds sprinkled on it. Once, you could see all of the junk I shoved aside in the mirror reflection. That was a lot of editing!

I want these next pages and my blog holiday tour to be inspirational for you, and I hope you enjoy "walking" through these homes. (After all, they cleaned and shoved the junk out of the way . . . just for you!) These homeowners have generously taken a few days out of their busy schedule and opened their front doors so I could share their spaces with you. I left every single one feeling inspired and amazed by their beautiful decorating and creative ways they made their homes ready for the holidays. So, grab your cup of hot cocoa as you page through each space and gather holiday inspiration!

ALISON SHERMAN HOUSE

RAISED ON A horse farm in rural Pennsylvania as a child, Alison immediately felt right at home in a 1930s polo barn and stables located in a quiet Chicago suburb. She knew it was the place she and her husband, Harry, could raise their children, Andrew and Emily, now college-aged.

As an interior designer, antiques dealer, and a love-of-all-things equestrian, Alison has transformed her home into a welcoming space with a traditional style, yet an "English country house" feeling. She and her business partner, Jenn Pattie, share a company called Blue Cardinal Antiques and Vintage located in a northern Chicago suburb and have found many of the equine accessories and details that reside in Alison's home while in search for items for their shop.

Alison's approach to decorating for the holidays includes lots of holiday greenery, vintage silver, and boxes of collected family ornaments. With evergreen as her favorite scent of the season, Alison loves decorating the fresh, green tree with her family; they add old, glass ornaments from her husband's grandmother's trees mixed in with newer ones, all while Christmas music plays in the background.

Not an area of her home is left untouched, and it is decorated with all kinds of holiday and winter decor. Alison says, "The last few years, I have collected old snowshoes, skis, and sleds that I love to dress up with fresh berries and pines and sit near the front and side doors during the holidays."

Some of her favorite holiday memories include childhood decorations. "I have some vintage glass Santa lanterns from when I was little. They are battery operated, and I remember my mom would light one and sit it next to my bed on Christmas Eve."

Making a relaxing and family-filled holiday is important to Alison and Harry. "My favorite tradition," says Alison, "would be that we all go downstairs together on Christmas morning. We start with the prizes left in our stockings at the mantel, then move to the gifts under the tree, taking turns to open each gift one at a time. It's a long, drawn out process, taking breaks for coffee and breakfast, but it makes the day and the process last a little longer. When the kids were little, they . . . ripped through their gifts at the same time!"

A WELCOMING bench offers guests a place to sit and remove their boots.

THIS ORIGINAL staircase is highlighted by greenery and framed vintage horse etchings. Alison added the well-used horseshoes and staged a pretty vignette in normally wasted space under the stairs.

IN NATURAL light, the stairway is just as pretty and details pop with a nice contrast between the woodwork and 75-year-old brick.

A VINTAGE trophy holds seasonal berries and boxwood.

THE CEDAR-PANELED
family room is Alison's favorite room to decorate because of the original fireplace and the warm tones of the paneling. It makes a cozy place to spend the winter.

ANTIQUE BOOKS paired with small silver cups, equestrian-themed silver boxes, and vintage bottlebrush trees make a pretty display.

THE KITCHEN island is an antique reproduction English hunt board. It has two marble inserts perfect for baking. Small holiday touches make the space cheery but still keep it a workable kitchen.

SKIRTS ON the island stools cleverly disguise places where one of their dogs chewed the legs as a puppy, but they also add a custom touch to the furniture pieces.

PEARS IN one of Alison's favorite silver compote bowls add a pretty touch to the kitchen.

THE KITCHEN, designed by Alison herself, has the advantage of being new but looks as though it always belonged there. Lamps and boxwood topiaries in vintage trophies flank the sink as a cozy yet elegant touch and a warm glow at night.

WITH ALISON'S love and talent for display, her built-in kitchen hutch is transformed by vintage ironstone, bottlebrush trees, and antique horse and equestrian memorabilia.

THE LONG hallway, fitted with old barn timbers that Alison bought off of Ebay, holds residence to a 10-foot long workbench. Imported from Hungary and refitted with an old barn beam base by a friend, it gets a natural touch of decorating with wood bowls, fresh greens, pine cones displayed in a vintage baby calf water trough, a vintage sheep shear sharpener, and her grandfather's sled.

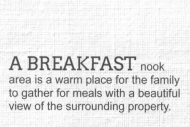

A BREAKFAST nook area is a warm place for the family to gather for meals with a beautiful view of the surrounding property.

172

A WELL-SET table with equestrian-themed dishware, vintage silver, and fresh flowers make a pretty table setting.

THE NOOK cabinet is an antique piece from the mid-1800s made from English oak. It has an older French clock built into the center cabinet space that conceals the original stone weights behind a long door. The shelves hold Alison's holiday collection of vintage Putz houses.

WHILE THE chairs are newer, they evoke the feel of an antique set with beautiful pastoral scenes painted in oil paints on the chair backs.

173

KEPT IN a traditional English style, the old tack room contains just a touch of holiday among tartan patterns, old plaid blankets, and vintage riding equipment.

DRESSED WITH
a mixture of vintage family ornaments and new, the fresh tree nestles perfectly in the floor-to-ceiling window.

THE COFFEE table gets a holiday vignette with touches of red.

THE OUTSIDE gets garlands and swags of greenery to complement the existing evergreens.

AN ANTIQUE hitch post stands sentry.

A CONCRETE jockey with a lantern welcomes guests.

ON THE expansive side porch, Hallie, the golden retriever, lounges on the best seat in the house.

JENNIFER ZURI HOUSE

NESTLED IN A clapboard farmhouse built circa 1875 in a cozy Illinois suburb, empty nesters Jennifer Zuri, her husband, Robert, and their rescue kitties live near the last train stop west of Chicago. Just a few blocks from the forest preserve and farm fields, they have the best of both worlds, able to enjoy the hustle and bustle of city life in nearby Geneva for shopping and dining and, when it suits them, retreat back to the refuge of their quiet town.

In a lovely Scandinavian cottage-style-inspired home filled with antiques and painted furniture, Jennifer loves the magic the holiday season creates and says, "I love the sparkle of my vintage ornaments collection and enjoy making the house look pretty." For her, decorating stirs cherished holiday memories: "My mother would spend an entire weekend decorating the house for Christmas. The carols would play on the old hi-fi, and I would always watch in amazement as she transformed our entire house. My dad's job was to decorate our 9-foot, white-flocked tree. We had a rotating Christmas tree stand that would play music."

Jennifer's children are now the proud owners of her mother's Christmas decorations, and Jennifer embellishes her own tree with a mixture of her grandmother's glass ornaments and vintage glass ornaments she finds while shopping at the flea market. She also loves displaying and mixing them with her vintage white ironstone and loves to use greenery, red berries, and dogwood twigs from the yard, with a candy cane thrown in for good measure.

The best parts of Christmas, however, are the traditions that come with it.

"My favorite tradition is one that we observed when I was a child. Before we open any presents, we read the story of Christ's birth from the Book of Luke in the Bible. I think it's important to remember the true meaning of Christmas amid all of the commercialism. Without Christ, . . . the holiday decor, baking, etc., means nothing."

VINTAGE
GLASS ornaments
are displayed in an
antique ironstone bowl
set on an old washtub.

GREENERY HIGHLIGHTS original molding and a hanging wooden sheep gets a pine collar, all while a rescued resident poses for a picture.

THE DINING room hutch, original to the house, gets a touch of holiday cheer with boxwood wreaths and pine boughs.

MINIATURE POINSETTIAS add a pop of holiday color to the hand-painted drop-leaf table.

ON A dining room buffet, chunky, iridescent glitter adds a touch of holiday glam.

A SIMPLE but pretty touch, French book pages are cut into a heart shape, sewn together on a sewing machine, and hung by a bit of twine.

A RECLAIMED wood shelf over the couch adds sparkle with bottlebrush trees and mercury glass.

VINTAGE BOTTLES and a distressed antique box add some interest to a painted coffee table.

POPS OF red in the room brighten the space.

EPSOM SALT–FILLED
mason jars tied with vintage-inspired mini-garlands and red berries add a pretty touch.

THE ORIGINAL staircase, which Jennifer revived herself by ripping out old 1980s pink carpet and painting the treads brown to stand up to the high traffic, is the perfect place for a basket of greenery and ornaments. The window gets a kiss of Christmas with a red-berried wreath and is the perfect space for her kitties to window gaze.

JUST INSIDE the welcoming entryway of one of the original doors is a place to take your boots off. Jingle bells at the top make a merry ring when guests enter.

184

A PAINTED crate holds candles and vintage bottles embellished with rusted metal hearts. A cluster of vintage-inspired bottlebrush trees add a touch of whimsy.

A DESK Jennifer painted and decoupaged herself has a joyful assortment of holiday items. The *ho ho ho* banner Jennifer made from plain white cards, stencils, and glitter. A vintage Santa image on an old pair of painted shutters make a festive display.

A COLLECTION of ironstone flank each wall on open shelving. Both are prettily decorated and styled with natural elements of greenery. The shelf to the right of the sink has a vintage cutting board dressed in a book page banner.

THE SHELF on the left side of the kitchen shows off many of Jennifer's loves: an amazing flea market vintage mirror, ironstone, and vintage glass ornaments that add a touch of color.

IN THE kitchen, blue-glass mason jars give a bit of color against ironstone plates. Greenery next to the sink and a Santa dish towel make for a cozy place to wash dishes.

185

A STAR hangs in the window with a wintery scene outside.

THE FAMILY room is a cozy place to cuddle up, decorated simply with a bowl of ornaments and just a few holiday touches. Jennifer transformed many of the pieces herself. Her talent for finding great flea market pieces and transforming them is apparent is this room with her cabinet and coffee table.

THE SHOWPIECE

of the kitchen, a built-in hutch with original handles, serves as the kitchens main storage. A merry banner adds a nice holiday greeting. Bursts of red show off the original handmade floor tiles.

JEANNE OLIVER
HOUSE

WITH A LOVE of history and family, artist and business-owner Jeanne Oliver and her husband, Kelly, make the most of the holiday season starting at Thanksgiving. "For me, Thanksgiving is not a time of stressing out on things; it's just a time to cook and be together." With an annual tradition of enjoying a home-cooked meal, taking a walk together on the hiking trails surrounding the Colorado mountains, and then coming home to settle down for a movie and homemade caramel corn make the holiday a special family time.

The day after, when most people are rushing around to find the best sale, Jeanne and her family head to a local tree farm and get a fresh tree. That event kicks off a season of getting ready for Christmas. "We use the time to prepare our hearts for Christ and our home for the holidays. We prepare for Advent by doing age-appropriate events all month long. Last year we did an 'Acts of Service' Advent tree. It included things such as helping another family with child care, shoveling neighbors' driveways and sidewalks, and looking for ways to thank people who have served our family, like the mailman and garbage man. We also did calls of kindness to people

in our lives and told them why we loved them. It's the little things."

Jeanne loves to decorate with vintage, well-loved finds. For her, the most important facet of decorating, holiday or not, is making her home comfortable and accessible for everyone. "I love when people come into our home and they say that everything feels warm and welcoming. It's because my stuff has already lived another life. I want things in our house people can touch, and I put it out knowing if it breaks, we are okay with it." Her biggest decorating influence was her Grandma Jeanne. "Her home was filled with art that she loved and connected with. She was a composer and singer and her house was always filled with music. When she brought us all together, she had a large table set with mismatched china and crystal, and 30 people sat around together. No one cared if everything matched. Everyone was just happy to be together."

Jeanne's approach to decorating for Christmas involves adding simple touches to what she already has. With a touch of European influence, and a desire to keep her home casual, holiday decor includes various greenery, ornaments collected over time,

French grain sacks, handmade artwork, ironstone, architectural accents, and natural fibers and textures.

Christmas Eve for the Oliver family involves having dinner together with extended family and Christmas Eve service. Afterward, the kids do a talent show, read their second-to-last Advent story, and open one gift from under the tree before bed. After the kids get to bed, they get a stocking set outside their doors, just like Jeanne's mom did for her and her siblings when they were little (which buys the grown-ups an extra hour of sleep in the morning). Christmas Day starts with opening gifts one at a time, and then after a treat of homemade cinnamon rolls, they spend the day with family, opening gifts and eating.

"Christmas for me is about faith and family; the more family in my house, the happier I am."

THE WELL-DRESSED HOLIDAY HOME

JEANNE'S FRESH tree involves well-loved ornaments collected over time.

THE TREE is adorned with a button garland.

AND THE tree is backed by a vintage ladder with antique grain sacks.

190

A HOLIDAY fabric banner adds to the everyday decor on the fireplace mantel, and a handmade wood star adds a rustic touch next to the framed grain sack.

THE MANTEL is simply dressed with vintage ironstone and fresh greenery.

BOXWOOD WREATHS add a touch of green, and red vintage grain sack pillows add a small pop of color.

THE WELL-DRESSED HOLIDAY HOME

191

JEANNE DRESSES her everyday space with simple touches and natural fibers.

A PAPER wreath made from vintage sheet music adorns an antique window in the music library.

KEEPING HER ottoman simple yet interesting, a tray holds vintage film canisters and fresh flowers in ironstone.

THE FRONT entry gets a jolly jingle when guests arrive from vintage French sleigh bells hanging on the back of the door.

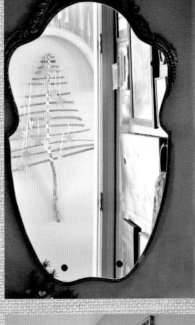

THE MAIN hallway holds this year's "Acts of Service" Advent calendar made by the family with found branches and paper stars.

THE WELL-DRESSED HOLIDAY HOME

LINEN STOCKINGS
and pinecones add a holiday touch
to the art-filled stairway.

AN UPSTAIRS window seat provides a peaceful place to sit and read.

THE UPSTAIRS hallway holds a collage with a hand-lettered sign by House of Belonging, a vintage picture of Jeanne's mother as a young girl, and other decorations to connect it all.

THE SEAT dressed in linen and ticking is a cozy place to enjoy artwork by Danielle Donaldson.

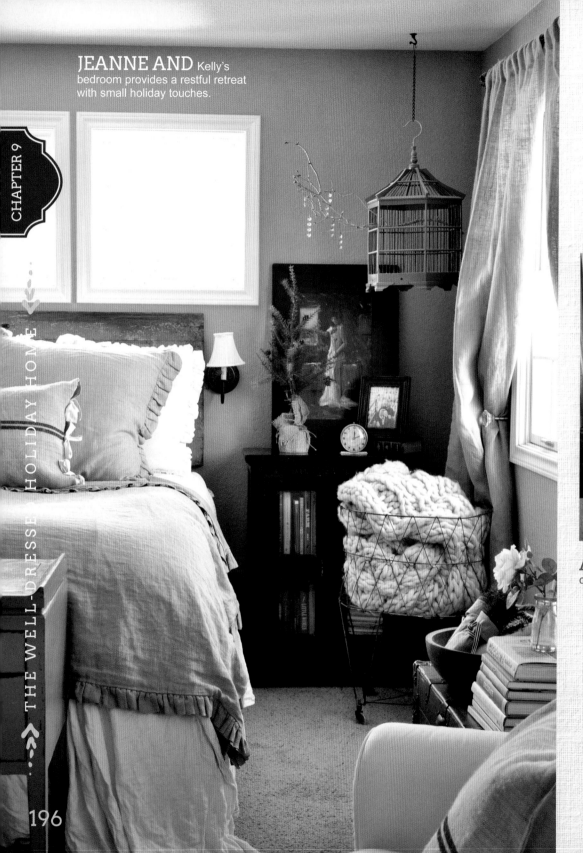

JEANNE AND Kelly's bedroom provides a restful retreat with small holiday touches.

AND IT includes a comfy place to sit and read.

196

A WOODEN bowl with grain sack bags and pine sprigs dress up a vintage trunk.

A LITTLE surprise hides behind a pillow on the headboard made from an old door.

ARTWORK FILLS every space, including a nightstand next to the bed. A small pine tree adds a rustic touch.

A ROLL of kraft paper celebrates "The First Noel" in French.

A MAIN gathering place for the family, the kitchen has simple decor and rustic touches to add to the much-used space.

A FARM print by Paige Knudsen adds to the kitchen decor.

SMALL TOUCHES
of red make the ironstone pop.

A CABINET backed in vintage sheet music holds vintage ironstone and is adorned by a tufted wool wreath.

THE VIEW gives a glimpse of the tree and living room decor.

MASON JARS for water and stockings with pine greens make for a pretty table setting.

THE TABLE is set with chalkboard paper, the image inspired by artist Karen Murray.

A VINTAGE apothecary cabinet holds art supplies.

JEANNE'S STUDIO space was at one time their dining room. Vintage notions and other bits and pieces stand in for ornaments.

MARK NORKAITIS HOUSE

WITH A GIFT for display and styling, Mark Norkaitis transformed his 1960s raised ranch from plain walls to a place full of amazing vintage and repurposed pieces with his signature industrial farmhouse style.

"This was my first home and I wanted to make it mine and put my stamp on it."

Those talents spilled over into opening his first store, Room 363, in downtown Naperville, Illinois, over a year ago and keeps his busy design business active.

"I've always wanted to open a store. I'd sold my repurposed furniture at flea markets and out of other people's stores for many years. I came up with the name Room 363 because it was my grandmother's address, [and she] raised me. I have the original house numbers on the shop's front door."

Christmas is a busy time for Mark between running the downtown holiday market just before Thanksgiving, making sure his shop is stocked and well-displayed for his customers, and helping his design clients. "I love helping my clients design their holiday decor. You get very personal with them around the holidays because they bring out their own traditions and heirlooms, and it's fun to incorporate that into their decorating."

In between all of the hastiness of the season, Mark still finds time to go all out at home with his own decor. "Now that I have my own home, I love to go all out. I love using unconventional things for my holiday decor, like succulents instead of pine branches, but I always have a real tree. I love the imperfectness of it."

He uses vintage and found items in his seasonal decorating, like vintage mercury glass and rustic industrial pieces. He also decorates with the items he buys for his own store, which is a second home for him. "I set up my store like a home and my displays reflect that. Christmas gives me a chance to completely transform my store from top to bottom. I am constantly changing things, so it's never the same store twice."

The Christmas holiday is also a time when Mark likes to visit with family or host a party with friends. Christmas Day is spent with cousins, exchanging gifts and having dinner. "The best part of the holiday season for me is seeing people happy. I love giving gifts and seeing how excited people get when they open them."

MARK'S LIVING room has an eclectic mix of vintage and found pieces. A vintage warehouse cart serves a second life as a heavy coffee table.

VINTAGE LOCKERS adorned with a driftwood wreath make a nice contrast of wood and metal.

VINTAGE SELTZER bottles on a mirrored tray are enhanced with vintage mercury glass ornaments and artificial snow.

A VINTAGE leather suitcase atop a dark wood console makes a great display opportunity with glass trophies, mercury glass, moss, and some glittery reindeer.

THE MASCULINE mix of leather with the industrial cart and stag head sculpture give a nice contrast with the vintage crystal light fixture.

MIXING FOUND and old items, Mark creates a unique display with a rusty found cast iron base, a vintage silver tray, and a pretty display of holiday items, including a cloche filled with vintage silver cups and succulents.

A REAL tree is the centerpiece of the living room and dining room combo.

THE TREE is filled with vintage ornaments and sprays of gold.

MARK'S BULLDOG, Ella, enjoys a comfortable seat.

MARK'S DINING

area's main wall holds a cabinet
he found at an old barn in
Hampshire, Illinois. It was a store
display until Mark was able to
have a house big enough to use it.

TOILE AND white dinner dishes mixed with vintage glassware and ironstone make a pretty table.

COLLECTED PASSIONATELY by his grandmother, cows hold a special place in Mark's decorating heart.

A BLACK chandelier dripping with crystals adds a glam touch to the room.

ESCHEWING THE traditional red and green Christmas decor, metal and silver make the table display with silver bells and metal elements.

A METAL galvanized tray with succulents and feathers gets a touch of color with red pears.

211

DENISE KNICKREHM
HOUSE

WHEN DENISE AND Greg Knickrehm were looking for a home near family to raise their small children, they looked for quite a while. When they first bought their 1909 Illinois farmhouse, it was nowhere near the shape it is today. Originally built as a single-family home and then eventually converted into a 2-flat in the 1930s, it had years of wear and tear and lacked updating. Many rooms had been added over the years and the house layout was chopped up. Denise's words were "This place is a mess."

They were able to purchase it from the original builder's daughter in 1989, who had seen the house being built by her father as a small child. She recalled seeing the horse-drawn wagons bring the lumber from 1907 to 1909. Denise and Greg knew right away that they would be converting it back to a single-family home as a place to raise their family.

They were able to keep a few elements, such as the original handmade staircase and inlay wood floors, but most of the house needed extensive repair. Greg, a general contractor and carpenter, gutted the entire interior and, under Denise's eye for design, made it into the beautiful home it is today. They converted rooms throughout the house, such as a 1st floor back bedroom into the eat-in kitchen. Greg found an old photo album of the home and realized that the first floor back bedroom was originally a screened-in porch area.

Denise was able to take her creative talent for display and design, along with Greg's help, and open her 1st business in 1998. Denise's current retail location, Denise's Adornments, is a popular shopping spot in Geneva, Illinois.

Denise's shop and her home go hand in hand. "I love decorating with new and vintage finds. I love following the trends but working the older elements back in. I won't have anything in my home that isn't in my shop and vice versa." Her home has a neutral, but warm, artistic, French farmhouse feel.

Even in her own home, Denise loves to decorate with themes, adding layers and details to every design, yet keeping other things simple. "Every year I buy what I call a 'Charlie Brown' tree. It's very airy and soft and open and doesn't take up the entire room."

Denise loves decorating her kitchen and dining room the most. These are her two favorite gathering places for her family and friends. Ironstone, vintage silver, and, this year, a music theme make these 2 rooms very special. "I love when everything flows and goes together."

Their dining room is the heart of their home every Sunday and on the holidays. "We love to have our family in our dining room. Greg made a special top for the dining room table that seats 16 people. We have a huge Italian family and get together every week. My mother always does the main course, and my siblings and I provide all the side dishes. Everything is a blessing in my life and is what God has given me. I could not have done it without Him, and I give all the credit to Him."

White Christ

A WELCOMING

entry by the original staircase
has a pretty chair where guests
can remove their snowy shoes.

A PRETTY paper-wrapped bottle and bits of silver add just a bit of neutral holiday sparkle.

DENISE CREATES an creative display with a vintage-inspired father tree and a reproduction Santos doll.

THE WELL-DRESSED HOLIDAY HOME

THE SHELVES on her zinc-topped table hold some of Denise's favorite elements: mercury glass and ironstone.

A DISTRESSED mirror, flanked by skis, wears a festive sign.

THE HUTCH in the living room has great storage and has had many incarnations. Now it has fun chalkboard door panels. The vintage window mounted to the top was found at an area estate sale and Denise added the vintage books that she painted white.

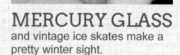

MERCURY GLASS and vintage ice skates make a pretty winter sight.

DENISE'S LOVE of pillows makes the couch a cozy place to sit.

THE "CHARLIE Brown" tree, adorned simply with white berries, vintage bead garland, and simple lights, is a perfect fit in the space next to her couch.

BIRCH LOGS rest upon a distressed wood box.

217

THE DINING room, this year inspired by a musical theme, is a favorite place for family gatherings.

A VINTAGE trombone, mercury glass, and sheet music make an easy centerpiece.

A VINTAGE violin and trumpet carry the music theme to a beautiful cabinet filled with many of Denise's favorite pieces.

A CHANDELIER is adorned with ribbons and greenery.

AN ANTIQUE door found at an estate sale is transformed with a wreath of greenery and noel letters.

219

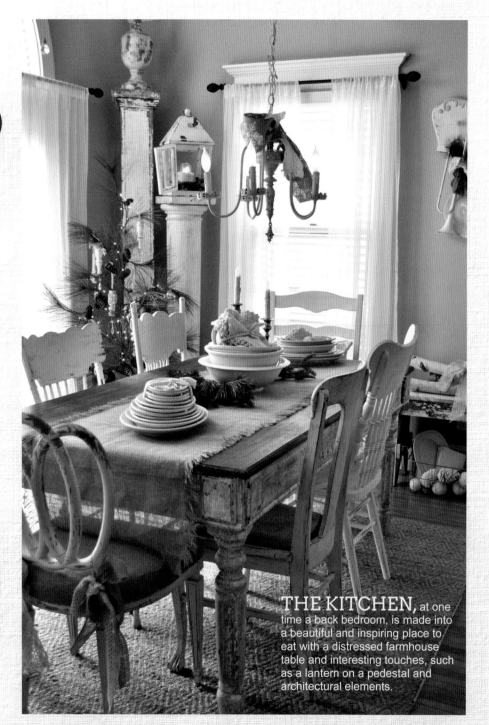

HER TABLETOP is waiting for service with ironstone and greenery.

THE KITCHEN, at one time a back bedroom, is made into a beautiful and inspiring place to eat with a distressed farmhouse table and interesting touches, such as a lantern on a pedestal and architectural elements.

NEXT TO the door, a trumpet stands at the ready to call everyone into dinner.

A HUTCH holds more pretty pieces, draped with a clever mitten garland.

A KITCHEN corner has a creative lamp shade filled with hanging vintage silverware. Mismatched china become instant decor.

221

A VINTAGE silver tray does double duty in the kitchen.

A TREE adorned with vintage spindles turned into ornament's warm up a corner space.

DENISE'S KITCHEN window has a beautiful view and Jolly old saint Nick.

HE WEARS a vintage sugar bowl lid as a chapeau.

TRACI TESSONE
HOUSE

FOR TRACI TESSONE, event planner and shop owner of Whimsy in Morris, Illinois, Christmas is her busiest yet favorite time of the year. In her shop, with the help of her mother, Debbie, she stocks the shelves with a rustic and elegant mix of crystals, burlap, and mercury glass. She also works as an event planner, setting up weddings, corporate events, and parties that make the season more festive. "I love doing weddings and corporate events around the holidays. They seem even more magical than normal with all of the lights and greenery and flowers."

At the end of a busy day, Traci escapes to her 1922 prairie-style home, originally built by a physician in the historic district of a Chicago southern suburb. She and her fiancé, Dan, purchased the home last year and have been slowly restoring it to its former glory with some 2014 updates. "The house wasn't like anything I had ever seen before because it had such character. The high ceilings and original woodwork were amazing, but I knew that it needed my touch. I could see the potential."

Reworking the layout by swapping a few doorways, adding some much-needed closet space, and replacing all of the hardwood floors added an instant update. She's also added her own touches, such as replacing the dated all-brick fireplace with a hand-carved limestone mantel, commissioned from a local craftsman; adding a mix of vintage and new lighting;

and incorporating many inexpensive flea market finds, like 25-dollar reupholstered chairs in the dining room.

With a romantic, glamorous, French-inspired style, Traci decorates for the holidays using the same approach she's uses in restoring her home. Many of her decorations are the things she carries in her store, but she adds in a few reproductions as well as authentic vintage pieces, taking her time to carefully select each one. "It's taken me a while to find everything for my home because I am very specific as to what I am looking for, and it's hard when you are dealing with one-of-a-kind pieces."

Traci also loves adding the unexpected surprise of fresh floral arrangements. "I think most people forget about fresh flowers at Christmas. I love having roses in my home for the holidays. I think they add a little romance in a small but wonderful way."

Her Christmas traditions involve the coziness of family gatherings and lots of food. She and her fiancé are looking forward to creating holiday traditions in their new home. "I can remember the feeling of my parents getting me really excited about Christmas Day and spending time with my cousins and getting together. I also think about all of the families that have lived here since 1922 and all of the holiday memories they have created, and I am hoping to create those same kind of memories."

FLANKED BY modern chairs and crowned with a flea market mirror, this limestone fireplace, inspired by an antique version, was hand carved by a local craftsman to replace outdated brick.

THE WELL-DRESSED HOLIDAY HOME

THE FIREPLACE display involves lots of fresh greenery, vintage elements, and fresh flowers.

WRAPPED PRESENTS in a vintage market basket make a merry display.

VINTAGE BROOCHES and faux greenery add a touch of glam to the twine-wrapped packages.

226

A FAUX tree in an urn gets a sparkle with mercury glass ornaments and jeweled snowflakes.

227

PRESERVED ORIGINAL
woodwork and doors make a statement
in the living room alongside flea market
portraits that become instant relatives,. .

THE OFFICE gets a touch
of elegance with a candelabra and
fresh flowers.

228

THE DINING room's long antique farm-style table is the perfect gathering place for Traci's entire family at the holidays.

A VINTAGE sled serves as a place to hold champagne and macaroons.

AS AN event planner, Traci loves to make a party table special.

VINTAGE SALAD plates find a new life as party plates.

229

THE STAIRWAY, original to the home, is a double stairway with a front and back side. The front side is accessorized with vintage skis and lanterns.

THE BACK staircase gets a vintage metal urn with fresh flowers,

ADORNED WITH
ice skates, this mirror reflects the original double staircase.

ICE SKATES sprayed with spray adhesive and sprinkled with natural mica glitter add a touch of glitz.

THE HALLWAY entry mirror was a flea market find with a plain back. Traci added the mirror.

UPSTAIRS, THE guest bedroom has a glamorous feel, with a full-size wall mirror and a reproduction tufted bed.

THE BEDSIDE nightstand also adds touches of glam and gold with a vintage frame that sets gold and crystal accents against a charcoal gray wall.

CUSTOM STOCKINGS
decorate the foot of the bed.

A VINTAGE dress form, clad in a gold wreath, and presents make a pretty display.

233

TRACI'S OWN bedroom has a romantic feel with an antique stone fireplace Traci found at an architectural salvage shop in the city.

A VINTAGE chair is a comfy place to curl up.

FRESH FLOWERS and an antique bust make an unconventional yet lovely holiday display.

JENNIFER RIZZO
HOUSE

NESTLED IN A suburb of Chicago with my husband, Nick, and our three children, I begin my Christmas decorating a few weeks before Thanksgiving. I host an annual housewalk on my blog, and it launches the first week of December, so I have to have everything photographed by December 1st and ready to go. That's fine with me though. I would rather be decorated for the holidays earlier instead of later. That means more time for enjoying Christmas!

Christmas decor is actually a year-round event for me. With my wholesale business, I have to have things ready for my retailers in October, so I am making holiday-inspired items in the middle of summer. I also normally do holiday shows up until December 1st and I have to have enough items for those too.

I create my holiday decor based on what love. My style is a bit vintage and a bit modern, with some artsy cottage thrown in. I create items based on those styles, and on my blog I like to show readers how they can also make their own home decor and crafts, because I think everyone's home should be different. It should reflect who lives there, what they love, and how they use their space.

Our space consists of a 1200-square-foot split-level that Nick and I have spent the last 13 years adding character to. I am actually an old-house person. I love all kinds of architecture, woodwork, and real wood floors. Any way I can add it in my house, I do.

The holidays give me the chance to be really creative with my decor. I love making new things for my home, getting the kids involved with crafting, and letting them express their decorating ideas. Our tree has my great aunt's vintage Shiny-Brite ornaments, other ornaments we've collected over the years, and all of the things the kids have made in school. I have a lot of wreaths made from paper plates and construction paper stars with pipe cleaners on my tree. I love it all.

Christmas is a family event with Christmas Eve service and three days of celebrating, eating, and enjoying time together. While I love the decorating and making part, family is my favorite part of the whole thing.

THE KITCHEN is the heart of the home. Once a cave with dark cabinets, it was remodeled in 2010. The light decor gives an opportunity to add different pops of color as the seasons change.

THE SINK gets a holiday touch with jingle bell garlands strung overhead, pops of red, and vintage Santa mugs with boxwood hair.

A NEW cabinet, painted to look old, holds the kid's cocoa mugs.

THE VIEW from living room to dining room gets dressed up with cedar greens and a handmade banner.

THE TREE gets decked with a mixture of vintage ornaments, handmade ornaments, and special memories made by the kids.

239

A PAIR of stag heads with branches and miniature ornaments keep holiday watch on the mantel.

THE FAUX FIREPLACE MANTEL was added a year ago to bring interest into the dining area, and a yarn fire keeps the family warm.

A CHANDELIER gets some boxwood swag and a little sparkle with vintage glass ornaments.

A STAG head over a vintage toolbox wears a boxwood wreath with a custom banner.

GREENERY, BIRCH candles, and a bit of glitter in a wood bowl make an easy centerpiece.

THE TABLE sports a handmade tablecloth and a touch of greenery.

THE OAK HOUSE

THE OAK HOUSE is a sweet cottage house in the suburbs. It's just a little three-bedroom ranch, but it has a ton of character. It was the perfect spot to use as a studio while creating this book and staying out of my family's way. We furnished it with thrift store finds, garage sale bargains, and even a few pieces dug out of family members' basements. I decorated it with many of the projects from this book and some products made by some very talented women. I wanted to give the Oak House a little bit of a spotlight since I spent so much time there!

THE TREE is dressed in a variety of ornaments, many of them made during the writing of this book.

A FUN REINDEER makes a nice display with paper pine trees and mercury glass on the hallway console table.

THE LIVING ROOM

opens up to the kitchen eat-in area. Garland is draped across a doorway we divided with repurposed stationary French doors.

THE KITCHEN ISLAND

shelf sports some fun bead holiday trees made from project leftovers! Painted with three colors of Miss Mustard Seed (MMS) milk paint and strung on bamboo skewers, they are standing in a base of foam balls left over from the snowball topiary project, a bit of clay around the edges from the hedgehog ornaments, and painted with MMS milk paint in linen with glitter on top.

THE MILK PAINT in

linen, purposely under-mixed to retain some small lumps, perfectly resembles a snowy texture when brushed on flowerpots or other surfaces.

A THRIFT store chair is dressed up with a pretty deer pillow by Craftberry Bush.

THE KITCHEN TABLE

gets decked out in birch-wrapped battery-operated candles.

AN OLD STEAMER TRUNK stands in for a coffee table and gets a little winter display of toy animals with faux snow in a vintage ceramic bowl.

THE MAIN living room couch makes a comfy place to sit when writing. A printed free-hand script Merry Christmas pillow by Dear Lillie adds a nice holiday touch.

ONE OF my favorite elements in the house, the faux mantel, was a favorite place to style and shoot. A Star of Wonder sign from Between You and Me Signs hangs above the jingle bell pom-pom trees and faux succulents in glittery flowerpots.

THE LIVING ROOM, with a fabulous southern exposure, had great light for shooting and made it a nice place to be all day.

JENNIFER RIZZO'S
2013 HOLIDAY HOUSEWALK

THESE ARE THE BLOGS that participated in my 2013 housewalk. These ladies continue to inspire me every day, no matter what the season. For some holiday cheer, you can stop by my blog, start the tour from the beginning, and "walk" through each home in order, or even visit the home tours from previous years. I have their everyday links included here so you can see what inspiring things they are doing year-round.

Jennifer Rizzo
jenniferrizzo.com

The Inspired Room
theinspiredroom.net

Thistlewood Farm
thistlewoodfarms.com

Jeanne Oliver
jeanneoliverdesigns.com

The Yellow Cape Cod
theyellowcapecod.com

The Handmade Home
thehandmadehome.net

Home Stories A to Z
homestoriesatoz.com

Eclectically Vintage
eclecticallyvintage.com

Four Generations One Roof
fourgenerationsoneroof.com

The Graphics Fairy
thegraphicsfairy.com

The Shabby Creek Cottage
theshabbycreekcottage.com

Dear Lillie
dearlillie.blogspot.com

Finding Home
findinghomeonline.com

French Country Cottage
frenchcountrycottage.
blogspot.com

Rusty Hinge
rustyhinge.blogspot.com

At the Picket Fence—Vanessa
atthepicketfence.com

SAS Interiors
sasinteriors.net

DIY Showoff
diyshowoff.com

Makely School for Girls
makelyhome.com

View along the Way
viewalongtheway.com

Between You and Me
betweenyouandmeblog.com

City Farmhouse
cityfarmhouse.com

Paige Knudsen
paigeknudsen.com

At the Picket Fence—Heather
atthepicketfence.com

The Shabby Nest
theshabbynest.blogspot.com

My Sweet Savannah
mysweetsavannah.blogspot.com

My Uncommon Slice of Suburbia
myuncommonsliceofsuburbia.com

Ella Claire
ellaclaireinspired.com

Unskinny Boppy
unskinnyboppy.com

Craftberry Bush
craftberrybush.com

Susie Harris
susieharrisblog.com

Flea Market Trixie
fleamarkettrixie.com

THE SPIRIT OF GIVING

AMONG THE GLITZ and bustle of the holiday season, there remains a special feeling, one that brings out the humanity of the holidays: the spirit of giving. It gives us a chance to reach out once a year and make someone else's life a little bit better. The best side effect of this is that we get the gift of joy in return. Wouldn't it be great if we could have that Christmas feeling all year? In that spirit, I wanted to share a list of some giving ideas. These are just a few out of the many. While many of these places and charities will take financial contributions, others would love your time or talent. And sometimes, giving just starts at home.

Feed My Starving Children
fmsc.org

Kiva—Loans That Change Lives
kiva.org

Living Water International
water.cc

Compassion International
compassion.com

The Special Olympics
specialolympics.org

Wounded Warrior Project
woundedwarriorproject.org

Red Cross
redcross.org

The Salvation Army
salvationarmyusa.org

Heifer International
heifer.org

The Grow Hope Foundation
thegrowhopefoundation.com

St. Jude Children's Hospital
stjude.org

These are just a few suggestions, but there are so many other ways to give and help beyond this list!

- Volunteer at or donate to a local food pantry.
- Donate to a winter coat drive or clothing drive.
- Help a local family in need.
- Volunteer for your local PADS or soup kitchen.
- Pick a present on a gift tree for someone in need.
- Shovel a neighbor's driveway.
- Offer to take an elderly neighbor, who doesn't drive, shopping.
- Make a meal for another family.
- Visit residents at a nursing home.
- Run an errand for a homebound person.
- Give pet food to the local animal shelter.
- Have a neighbor or friend without local family over for dinner or to share the holiday.
- Leave a surprise gift on a friend's doorstep.
- Give a grocery gift card anonymously to a struggling family.
- Make a phone call to someone you know might be struggling this season.
- Offer to babysit a few hours for a mom with young children.

SUPPLIES AND RESOURCES

HERE IS A GLIMPSE of where you can find some of the supplies and products featured in the projects and homes in this book. Many supplies are seasonal, and your store may not carry them. But they can be found by searching online as well.

Dick Blick

drafting tape

lino carving kit

lino carving blocks

fabric screen printing ink

ceramic paint pens

glitter

multipurpose glue

white tacky glue

gold and silver pipe cleaners

wood craft rounds

air-dry and paper-based clay

Michael's

paper-based clay

Snow-Tex dimensional snow medium

acrylic craft paint

24-carat gold spray paint

looking glass (mercury glass) spray paint

stamps

StazOn ink

glitter tape

craft punches

small Styrofoam balls

hot glue

glue guns

Joann Fabrics

felt

felt/fabric glue

upholstery webbing

burlap

yarn

sequin trim

plain tea towels

plain tote bags

plastic sheeting

quilt fabric

sheet moss

Hobby Lobby

pom-poms

jingle bells of various sizes

white tacky glue

hot glue

glue guns

acrylic craft paint

spray paint

wreath forms

paint brushes

sheet moss

reindeer moss

gold wire

letter and number stencils

ceramic paint pens

yarn

adhesive shelf liner

wood craft rounds

air-dry and paper-based clay

Mod Podge decoupage medium

Saveoncrafts.com

birch sheets

moss sheets

Createforless.com

Snow-Tex dimensional snow medium

paper-based clay

air-dry clay

Vintage Graphics for Projects

thegraphicsfairy.com

Text/Fonts for Projects

dafont.com

Other Art Resources

Karen Murray
www.papercraftmemories.com
wordartbykaren.etsy.com

Paige Knudsen
paigeknudsen.com

Citrasolv

citrasolv.com

Vintage and French Goods

dreamywhitesonline.com

jeanneoliverdesigns.com

frenchlarkspur.com

Handmade Pillows

dearlillie.com

craftberrybush.com

Milk Paint

missmustardseedmilkpaint.com

Lettered Message Signs

betweenyouandmeblog.com

thehouseofbelonging.com

Farmhouse Style and Home Decor

perfectlyimperfectshop.com

Shops Mentioned in This Book

room363.net

denisesadornments.com

whimsydecor.blogspot.com

bluecardinal.blogspot.com

jeanneoliverdesigns.com

ACKNOWLEDGMENTS

I COULD NEVER HAVE DONE this book on my own. There was so much more involved behind the scenes than just me, a camera, and many trips to the craft store. I had an entire support team of love and encouragement behind me.

I want to first thank God for working every day in my life and working through me to create an entire book! I couldn't have been able to create this amazing blessing without Him!

Thank you to my husband, Nick, and my beautiful girls for standing beside me, lifting me up, and putting up with all of the times I had to serve them frozen food or have dinner delivered.

Thank you to Cedar Fort Publishing and the amazing people who used their amazing talents to work so hard for this book: Haley Miller, Whitney Lindsley, Angela Baxter, and Deborah Spencer.

Thank you to my mom for supporting me and providing me with endless hours of childcare. Dad, I know you're watching and smiling. And thank you to my extended family including siblings, cousins, and in-laws for supporting me.

And for your love, support, and encouragement:

Jeanne Oliver, Mary Mansfield, Nicola McGarry, Leslie Vasich, Eileen Duban, Jim Bonk, Anne Schrieber, Kelly Elko, Gina Luker, KariAnne Wood, the Ruszay family, Karen Watson, Collette Heimberg, and the Bonk family.

My contributors for picking up the slack: Jen at City Farmhouse, Kristen at EllaClaire, Angela at Number Fifty-Three, Jennifer at Town and Country Living, and Jamie at So Much Better with Age.

All of my retailers for selling my designs and goods and then asking for more . . . and my customers for buying them!

The guys at the HFD . . . it was all a part of the journey and I could have not gotten here without you.

The Wednesday morning ladies group . . . your prayers were well used.

And last but certainly not least, my blog family of readers, commenters, and fans. You guys are the ones who have been hanging in there with me through good and bad the last 6½ years, and I am blessed to have you.

THANK YOU to these wonderful people for opening up their homes and providing their amazing talents, products, resources, and services.

Alison and Harry Sherman
thepolohouse.blogspot.com

Alison Sherman and Jenn Pattie
Blue Cardinal Antiques & Vintage
bluecardinal.blogspot.com
531 Bank ln.
Highwood, IL
847-710-0801

Bill and Linda Curran

Bill and Susanne Murray

Denise and Greg Knickrehm
Denise's Adornments
denisesadornments.com
221 S. 3rd street
Geneva, IL 60134
630-232-8855

Jason and Becky Gersakey

Jeanne and Kelly Oliver
jeanneoliverdesigns.com
jeanneoliver.ning.com

Jennifer Holmes
dearlillie.blogspot.com
dearlillie.com

Jennifer Zuri
Town-n-Country-Living.com

John and Kathy Kelly

Karen Watson
The Graphics Fairy
thegraphicsfairy.com

Kathy Kelly and family

Kimberly Fenelon-Justus
serendipityrefined.com

Marian Parsons
missmustardseed.com

Mark Norkaitis
Room 363
room363.net
232 S. Washington
Naperville, IL 60540
630-778-0363

Nicola McGarry and family

Tara Lowry
betweenyouandmeblog.com

Traci Tessone
whimsydecor.blogspot.com
106 W Washington St.
Morris, IL 60450
815-513-5600

The Vasich family

INDEX

JENNIFER RIZZO

JENNIFER RIZZO is an artist and designer who owns Jennifer Rizzo Design Company. She loves designing home decor and artwork. She has been wholesaling and retailing her items for over six years and sells her handmade home decor creations in boutiques and retailers across the United States. She has been featured in and produced projects for publications such as *Country Living*, *Romantic Homes*, and *Somerset Home*. She teaches art and handmade classes, speaks about creative living, and writes about DIY and artful living on her popular lifestyle blog www.jenniferrizzo.com.

She is nestled in the Chicago 'burbs with her husband, three kids, and lots of projects waiting to be worked on.